I AM A WESTERN OCEAN MARINER

J.S. Earl

To Mo

Best Wishes

Joe. x

ISBN 978-1-905553-30-3

Published and Printed by
Dolman Scott Ltd
www.dolmanscott.com

I AM A WESTERN OCEAN MARINER

A COLLECTION OF SEAFARING VERSE

(AND OTHER STUFF)

In special memory of my brother John 1930 - 2004

A fine seaman and Bo`sun, he served on many ships during his time at sea, among them were the:
M.V. King Steven, M.V. Baron Inverclyde,
S.S. Consuelo, M.V. Sacremento, S.S. Merchant Knight,
S.S. Dorrington Court, S.S. Beechwood, S.S. Rinaldo,
S.S.Athel Knight, S.S.Ariosto, S.S. Saint Thomas,
and the *Sir Arthur Kennedy*.

Contents

MY POETRY

I know it isn't poetry – it isn't even prose
I'm really very sorry if it travels up your nose
Shall we call it doggerel?
What do you suppose?

THE WESTERN OCEAN

I’m a Western Ocean mariner and I’ll tell you if I can,
Of awesome winter weather encountered here by man,
The seas build up with fury over miles of storm tossed waves,
Hulls of ships are pounded and steering misbehaves.

Clouds are tattered rags amid the frequent squall,
Merging with the streaking peaks many storeys tall,
The air it feels like buckshot in the form of spray,
Wind is banshee howling, through rigging in the way.

A `hogging and a `sagging we ride the raging main,
Fore and aft with shaking mast the vessel wracks with strain,
Rolling and a pitching in vast and lengthy swells,
Thundering seas crashing down filling up the wells.

We dare not run before it - we’d poop our stern asunder,
We must not run along it - we’d roll ourselves right under,
The motion of a corkscrew she spirals up and round,
Crashing into head seas with a `whoomping` sound.

Half a mile from crest to crest in rolling hills of brine,
Ship trembling now but climbing - only just in time,
Arriving on a summit, we take a diving plunge,
Dropping down into a trough with stomach churning lunge.

The stern would lift, engine race, the screw would clear the water,
Speeding in its freedom - vibrating through the quarter,
Shovelled up the hawse pipes, a green sea thumps the prow,
Shooting tons to leeward off the flooded bow.

Battened down and hove-to waiting out the weather,
Standing tricks and watches working there together,
A sturdy ship beneath me and doughty crew beside,
A Western Ocean seaman takes it in his stride

I AM NO SAILOR

The crew are just fine on their ship of the line,
Rolling and pitching in seas,
While making headway in salty blown spray,
I'm retching on hands and my knees.

She's sheering and shaking as homeward she's making,
Taking it all in her stride,
While I'm in the bog as sick as a dog,
Regretting this nautical ride.

I'm the colour of green in a bouncing latrine,
My eyes all streaming and red,
There is a long way to go - I'd rather not know,
As I puke and wish I was dead.

PQ 17

A convoy bound for Russia in July of '42
Gathered off old Reykjavik in Iceland's summer hue,
Thirty five big freighters laden with supplies
Sailing in the midnight sun – some thought it was unwise.

Still a perilous journey, rolling like a log,
With the sea spray freezing and banks of icy fog,
Across the Arctic Ocean all without a lee,
Toward the North of Norway to the Barents Sea.

Steaming ever watchful, ticking off the hours,
Shepherded by Navy ships with their fighting powers,
Including three destroyers guarding yet again,
Stores to move an army of fifty thousand men.

Back at home in London the Admiral Dudley Pound,
Sent a message to his Navy "You will withdraw Westbound",
The cause of this dire action to the Admiral was plain,
The Germans sailed their surface ships and Tirpitz was to blame.

The stunned escort Commander – his orders must obey,
Turned his men at full speed and sent them all away,
From his cruisers to the convoy the signal lamp did chatter,
"Sorry lads to leave you but convoy now must scatter".

Though Tirpitz left her moorings – there wasn't any threat,
Unhappily, the power that be, didn't know that yet,
Thus we had the convoy dispersed and all spread out,
At the mercy of the Luftwaffe and U-boats there about.

Now the deadly onslaught on July the fourth began,
The sinking of the Carlton, William Hooper, Zaafaran,
Paulus Potter, River Afton, Navarino, Honomu,
The Pancraft and the Earlston, Dan Morgan just a few.

Many ships were doomed – they numbered twenty four
With their vital cargoes sent to the ocean floor,
Misleading information meant brave men went to die,
Left without protection, knew not the reason why.

(Just part of the cargoes lost on the PQ17 included 3,350 motor vehicles, 430 tanks, 210 bombers, radar sets and ammunition. The exact number of men lost is not known).

MERCHANT SEAMEN

In War and peace they plied their trade,
Over the angry seas ,
Remember them as here you stand,
Beneath these placid trees.

Inscription on the Merchant Navy Memorial, Welsh Back Bristol.

MY HEROES

Speak not to me of Heroes unless they served at sea,
Men that have the Nelson touch - they're the ones for me,
They sailed the coast of England and all the globe around,
Saviours of our country that our blue lanes surround.

Whether past or future - Admiral or not,
Takes a special breed of man to take a sailors lot,
From wooden ships and iron men sent out to explore,
To keeping lifelines flowing in desperate times of war.

Oiling wheels of commerce fighting all the way,
Engaging with the enemy - the weather everyday,
Steaming in the convoys risking life and limb,
Or sailing bowsprit under at a typhoon's whim.

The hardy Western Ocean men you cannot disregard,
Or those that manned the tea clippers reefing on the yard,
Maybe in a submarine in claustrophobic space,
Perhaps upon an oil rig in a God forsaken place.

The pilots and the tug men that work the clock around,
At the end of voyages docking safe and sound,
Lifeboat crews and fishermen - all that do their share,
So take me back to sea boys - my heroes are all there.

BILL

One thousand miles from nowhere, a tinfish hit its mark
Its target was a British ship which foundered in the dark,
The crew were killed or injured and could not stay afloat,
Just four of them were able to make it to a boat.

They watched their ship go down, upon a Christmas eve,
In a state of shock pondering their reprieve,
There they stayed and suffered - in tropic heat they sweltered,
Death was standing by them - no comfort and unsheltered.

They finished all the bully beef and licked the milk cans dry,
One of them had died by now as forty days went by,
The remaining three were skeletons - living, just - but weak,
When picked up by the Navy could not stand or speak.

Three weeks on, saw them home - recovered bit by bit,
Replacing all their papers and Merchant seaman's kit,
One man was a mate of mine - let's just call him Bill
I'd met him there when rescued and very very ill

I thought I'd go and see him - take him to a pub,
Found his home in Liverpool and thereby lies the rub,
I knocked the door - his wife came out - told me that her Bill,
Bored with life ashore - refused to bide there still.

Ten days only he was home - then he said to me,
"I'm signing on again Old Girl" and went off back to sea."

Derived from a story told on the radio in one of the ever-memorable postscripts narrated after the B.B.C. news during 1941 by Frank Laskier - from his book of transcripts; My Name Is Frank

THE VINDICATRIX

Have you heard of Mrs Drysdale? - no reason why you should,
Unless you were a Vindi Boy recalling pretty good,
She's the smartly painted figurehead from your training ship,
Which started life in `93 down a launching slip.

Many thousand old boys have memories of her,
Men from Vindicatrix I'm sure will all concur,
Training there was tough, discipline a blast,
But the making of a seaman from boy to man at last.

They came, perhaps, from cities, a village or the plough,
And grew aboard the Vindi - with Drysdale on the bow,
Learning by the hard times, the hunger and the strife,
The hale and hearty culture and friends made there for life.

The lads were taught seafaring ways, `afore they went abroad,
Instilled in them the values, that helped them stand assured,
Eventually they sailed away, each with doughty crew,
Plying trade around the world where the `duster` flew.

They joined the ranks of steadfast men, who kept our commerce flowing,
Withstanding foe and stormy seas when the winds were blowing,
All for one and shipmates - when the devil knocks,
Stemming from their early days hard by Sharpness docks.

A kindred spirit bonds them, by sailing `neath the stars,
The sea their life and laughter when living under spars,
Boldly then, they stood the worst, in peace, or war convoys,
Nothing less would one expect - from Vindicatrix boys.

THE `COAL SCUTTLE` BRIGADE

The war was on our doorstep, the Germans sent us hell,
With their mines and bombers - torpedo boats as well,
Through the E - boat Ally, our colliers braved the way,
Steaming round to London, mostly every day.

They came in coastal convoys from seaports in the north,
Vital coal the cargo - from Tyneside and the Forth,
Providing crucial energy for City and the Shires,
As well as fuel for railways, and domestic fires.

En route to power stations, with jetties on the river,
Thirty thousand tons a week they needed to deliver,
A voyage runs to Fulham and many a southern quay,
Like the one at Brunswick wharf and pier at Battersea.

Ships sent down from Welsh ports also braved onslaught,
Through the Hell Fire Corner making life so fraught,
Sitting ducks for E- boats from Goodwin Sands to Dover,
Fifteen guns at Cape Gris Nez lobbing shells right over.

Hardy Merchant seamen - experienced sea dogs,
Butted `tween the sand bars in frequent local fogs,
Defiantly they battled on, fought the harsh oppression,
While losses were horrendous in day and night aggression,

Through the wartime years, the colliers sailed the coast,
So many killed or injured giving their utmost,
These our unsung heroes of this battle of the sea,
I only hope you Southerners enjoyed your cup of tea!

WE COULD MAN A BATTLESHIP

(The Merchant Navy Association.)

We could man a battleship, we could sail a scow,
Association members have not forgotten how,
We still remember Morse code and streaming of the log,
How to sail the wide world and navigate in fog.

We can wield a trusty sextant and box the compass round,
Pull a heavy piston to a chain block's rattle sound,
We could feed all hands, with plenty left for suppers,
Though the vessel's pitching and rolling to the scuppers.

We could anchor anywhere and count the shackles home,
Cleaning up, outward bound, use the holy stone,
Rig a stage or boson's chair - throw a heaving line,
Most things being nautical we can do just fine.

We bade farewell to splicing and seamen's` work by hand,
The cranky coal fired engine and steam emitting gland,
But one thing may be lacking in these modern days,
Is how to work the Sat. Nav. or `push the button` ways.

So we sit back in retirement and think of olden times,
Like sweating in the tropics supping juice of limes,
Perhaps a Russian convoy freezing half to death,
As well as mighty hurricanes that take away one's breath
.

Still, we know it's over as we contemplate a glass,
Nothing like a full life to make regrets so sparse,
We are baffled by technology and systems that are new,
This ever-ready bunch of ours - this out of date old crew.

S.T.V. ROYSTON GRANGE

Worse things happen at sea they say – worse things happen at sea,
In `72 this came true with the tanker *`Tien Chee`*,
Within dense fog near the River Plate, she collided with a freighter,
Petrol gushed from shattered tanks exploding seconds later.

The other ship the *`Royston Grange* ` in fatal rendezvous,
Lost seventy four razed on her - all passengers and crew,
Full cargo holds of butter ignited overall,
Fused in mighty fireball that left no chance at all.

Ten thousand tons of vessel went up in lethal blaze,
No time then for rescue or warning sound to raise,
Montevideo close at hand, bodies still entrapped,
The Houlder`s ship towed away and later on just scrapped.

By the Tower of London – in All Hallows Church,
There is a stained glass window - if carrying out research,
In commemoration colour with burning red repands,
Depicting Royston Grange in memory of all hands.

Worse things happen at sea they say,
Worse things happen at sea…..

THE TREGENNA

Picture yourself in a convoy on a wild September day,
Astern of a ship named *Tregenna* – just three cables away,
She's steaming along at eight knots, with a cargo of steel in the hold,
Pitching heavy in head seas, into the spray and the cold.

When all of a sudden a U-boat dodging the escort screen,
Fired a salvo of tinfish, tracking through fast… unseen,
This lethal spread of torpedoes became *Tregenna's* death knell,
Just as her bow descended, headlong into the swell.

It was a fatal plunge that the ship was in,
Breached below her deck-line, through the plates so thin,
Her freight stowed heavy and low, beneath an empty space,
Quickly led to foundering, when water took its place.

The ocean rushed in so quickly, leaving no time to prepare,
She dived on her nose and kept going, stern shot high in the air,
The watch on the bridge jumped clear, perchance or not to drown,
Only four abandoned her - as the ship went down.

Now you have the story when in the vessel astern,
Two minutes it took to reach there, horrified to learn,
There was no sign of *Tregenna* - just Atlantic waves,
Thirty three men within her, bound to deep sea graves.

Sinkings were so frequent on a convoy's run,
But our merchant seamen still defied the Hun,
One reason why our monument stands there to remember,
Is for the likes of these men, who died here that September.

The Tregenna sailed from Halifax in convoy HX71 on 5th. September 1940.
On September 17th. The U-65 fired the torpedoes that struck the Tregenna just as the ship pitched forward. She did not recover and stood vertically, briefly, before sinking. She was 413ft. long carrying 8,500 tons of steel
This catastrophe was observed by men of the Filleigh who were in station less than two minutes travelling time directly astern of Tregenna.
According to the 2nd. Mate, she had sunk in less than forty seconds. There were four survivors.

ALFIE AND ME

Alfie and me on the poop deck jawing about the war,
We didn't see it coming – we never heard a roar,
Tin fish blew our tanker up, then it wasn't there,
Found ourselves in the 'oggin after flying in the air.

The sea afire and burning – we were in the clear,
Just me and him went diving – nobody else was near,
Alfie found some flotsam – his arm hooked round a spar,
He could hear me swearing – I wasn't away too far.

He flippered his way towards me and grabbed me by my shirt,
Bent me to the timber – told him I was hurt,
"*Not a night for swimming*" he bellows with a grin,
"*Not*" says I just gasping *"wiv arf me ribs stove in"*.

I feared of what would happen, striving to stay afloat
Atlantic cold – near freezing and oil had reached my throat,
Alfie was out of the stoke hold – a stubborn buggar was he,
(I was one of the deck crowd, he had cottoned on to me).

For hours and hours he held me, 'most drowned and body aching,
Without a doubt he saved me, through the dawn a breaking
I was finished with engines, ready to chuck it all in,
Alfie it was that chivvied, with jokes as bad as sin.

I figured we should pray, in case we might survive,
But he didn't think that prayers would keep us both alive,
He said he knew no hymns, 'cus he'd never shipped on liners,
What he reckoned was – a collection for the miners.

Alfie weren't religious – he didn't have to be,
Just a Merchant Seaman living his life at sea,
One o' them men that won't give in – fighting 'till the end,
Lucky for me an' proud to be his mucker and a friend.

By and by a ship came up with a Navy navigator,
He'd steamed away to chase a sub but marked our spot for later,
There's only me and Alfie came through that mighty blast,
I spoke a silent prayer – for the mate who held me fast.

(From a true yarn told to me by Alfie's mate some fifteen years after the event).

THEY BORE THE BRUNT.

They sailed the seas to bear the brunt,
They steamed the courses laid,
Ten thousand miles their battle front,
Unbacked and undismayed.

Fine seamen these of our great race,
From your seaport or town,
They risked their lives with danger faced
Until their ship went down.

Remember them - they held the line,
Won freedom on the way,
Remember them - their life was thine -
On merchant navy day

FROM A RUSSIAN CONVOY

A cargo ship is steaming into the Bearents Sea,
Heaving, rolling, pitching, bound for Murmansk quay,
The previous night in awful plight, her convoy had been scattered,
Best-laid plans are history now as slim defence is shattered.

Arctic storms are frequent, floating mines abound,
Dodgy is the compass and ice floes all around,
Watching out for U - boats and torpedoes mortal run,
The only means of fighting - an antiquated gun.

The fog and snow - sixty below, in the freezing winds,
Sodden clothes and eyes are froze staring through the `bins,
High on deck lifelines rigged to struggle fore and aft,
Shipping seas all over, in deeply laden draught.

Through a gap a spotter plane at distance overhead,
Homing in the Stukas with spectre of bloodshed,
Vital cargo must get through - vehicles and tanks,
Ammo with the aircraft and stores for army ranks.

Seldom war quite like it, in all our history,
Knowing that our chances are only two from three,
Even berthed in Russia the bombs fall every day,
Twenty minutes flying time - the Germans have their way.

There is no special thanks, for this appalling run,
Facing awful weather and unremitting Hun,
Many Merchant Seamen never make it through,
Giving all for Country in this year of `42.

BATTLE OF THE ATLANTIC

In '42 – part through the war – where the longest battle played,
Our lifeline 'cross the Ocean in crucial balance swayed,
Nine thousand men, five million tons, never made it home,
This appalling tally, in that twelve months alone.

There was no place to hide in a floating steel abode,
The Hun had found and cracked it – our secret Navy code,
They lay across our bow – they knew whereof our route,
Loaded up with tin fish waiting there to shoot.

An order spoke from Hitler to Dönitz and his crew,
Sink the ships and lifeboats – kill survivors too,
These infernal words, to his U boats went …………
Rescue none – leave none afloat – the ghastly message sent.

Dauntless merchant seamen, sailed and scorned their fear,
For weeks on end the persevered, vicious death was near,
Slow and easy targets for the Kriegsmarine,
Launching their torpedoes in day and night routine.

These lethal hungry wolf packs, lurking out of sight,
Delivered mortal damage in this underhanded fight,
Convoys crossed the 'black pit' beyond the reach of planes,
Contending with the enemy and awesome hurricanes.

Our mariners endured – steaming through Hell's gate,
Powerless and helpless, to know their own ship's fate,
Difficult and dangerous, also poorly paid,
With stubborn sense of purpose they carried on their trade.

In '43, eventually, the tide was slowly turned,
Brave escorts grew formidable with tactic lessons learned,
Aircraft stretched from Iceland flying to the hilt,
Long range Liberators with radar newly built.

Canadians and Yanks, toiled to aid us through,
Supporting our red duster and turning of the screw,
All we have of freedom that we use or know,
Seamen helped to bring it, many years ago.

A SEAFARER`S PRAYER

Oh Lord above please keep an eye,
On all seafarers sailing by,
Some are soft or hard as nails,
But seek thy love when all else fails.

If while steaming shore to shore,
We lose the fight - to endure....
Certain perils day or night,
Then we pray to see the light.

We may be selfish, scared, exposed,
Humbled now by human woes,
Since passing by the harbour trees,
To facing death in endless seas.

If by fate our days are numbered,
Set heaven's course unencumbered,
Whether sinner, near or far,
Please guide us Lord, across the bar.

SPIKE & FID

A Sailor born, a Sailor bred,
A tough Shellback was our man Fred,
His favourite job stood him apart,
Expert splicing was his art.

Rope or wire it didn't matter,
Though `tis said he chose the latter,
He wormed and parcelled with the lay,
A perfect job in every way.

Serving tight with marline spun,
Grinning proud when all was done,
Alas one night he died in bed,
No more tucks for dear old Fred.

At his graveside stood his wife,
Thought perhaps he'd miss his knife,
Unscrewed then his coffin lid,
Then added too his spike and fid.

THE LAST REUNION - SHIPS

You've heard of Para Handy and his Puffer - *Vital Spark,*
Of course you know of Noah and the grounding of his *Ark,*
All vessels have a life and time - with natural will and ways.
Rolling and a`pitching when steaming through the waves.

You may ask the veterans in Liverpool's fair city,
Gathered here in final year - to a band's last ditty,
Time has gone but memories long while shell-backs are alive,
They'll speak of ships on danger trips that helped them to survive.

Some craft faced mortality in Western Ocean's roar,
Waiting death from U-boats in that cruel and mighty war,
`Till the deadly tin-fish, met them on the flanks,
Of liners and the escorts, the tankers and the tramps.

Some torpedoed in their prime, plates all ripped and tearing,
Other ones grew old and carried on seafaring,
They died a death or lived a life, maybe badly mauled,
Flying our Red Duster where ever duty called.

From the wallowing rusty bucket to the liner up ahead,
Someone somewhere loved `em with grieving eyes so red,
We do remember those ships that steamed along in lines,
They saved our land when needed, in dire and desperate times.

After sterling service and life that's very hard,
Her decks and loosened rivets met the breakers yard,
They weathered all the storms - now just cast aside,
But like the men that manned `em, bless `em all with pride.

There is no stone on a ship's big tomb
Just names marked down in the Admiral's room
Their only cross on a chart prostrate,
A pencilled fix to point their fate.

SUZY SAN

We loaded coal at Dunston and sailed for Chittagong
A voyage fraught with monsoons made it wet and long
Our cargo then discharged we steamed up the river Hooghly
Dry docked in Calcutta, proceeded back to sea
Sailing to Malaysia – anchored five miles off Dungun
Prior to loading iron ore at the land of rising sun
Arriving then in Kobe and drawing twelve week's pay
Girding up our loins for a pleasant shore side stay.

There was a tempting place it wasn't very far
With a mate I entered and ordered from the bar
As beautiful young ladies sedately served our beer
Upped and clinked our glasses to wish each other cheer
We paired off very quickly as the girls imparted more
Turns out the staff were orphans who slept there on the floor
Wc treated them when time was called to a near hotel
(Not only just our two, but another three as well).

We frolicked in a deep bath, put dressing gowns to wear
Sat cross-legged on the floor to choose the menu there
The main dish – sukiyaki, a meaty, spicy, stew
Washed down with lots of saki – made a happy crew
I took my girl upstairs – I called her Suzy San
Leaning on my arm she called me her Sailor Man
Took my time, caressed her from earlobes to the knee
She responded beautifully, made love right back to me.

Nothing in young manhood surely could surpass
The lusty, loving while with my oriental lass
Night time was sheer heaven with hours of ecstasy
Five days of pure passion 'tween Sexy Sue and me
She was so very cuddly and answered every whim
Suzy was so fabulous, to leave her was a sin
Time to go we battened down hammered wedges in the lugs
Singled up the mooring ropes, blew loudly for the tugs.

Thirty tearful women waved our crew away
Suzy San among them, wishing my return one day

When we dropped the pilot and settled on our course
The Captain turned to the Mate, his voice was rather coarse
"I know they dropped the atom bomb, I know the reason why
That's the fault of war mate – so many people die
But can I believe in God – is there no redeemer ?
When you think of girls like those ……that died at Hiroshima".
Almost as told to me by my brother John,
S.S. King Stephen circa 1949.

SOMETIMES

Sometimes a ship's at anchor riding in a lee,
Sometimes a ship's just steaming – clear and running free,
Sometimes a ship's in dry dock a`mending of her plates,
Sometimes a ship's near hove-to, in a gale across the Straits.
Well that's the way my love-life, mirrors in a fashion,
Sometimes quiet and cosy, past a night of passion,

Sometimes it's a chasing thrill when the evening's going well,
Sometimes recuperating and relaxing for a spell,
Sometimes there's an argument when eyeing up another,
Then I find an even keel and go and visit Mother!

BATTERY POINT

On Battery Point at Portishead there's a slab of Portland stone,
It's there in dedication - standing proud alone,
To seamen of the west country who sailed here close to shore,
On voyages of history in times of peace and war.

These sterling men of England cast off from local quays,
Roved to far flung countries across the seven seas,
Outward bound they passed this spot over sands of time,
Battened down, Bristol style, vessels in their prime.

They went to join the convoys with danger at the fore,
Or missions of discovery when sent out to explore,
Flew the old red ensign wherever they were going,
Kept our lifelincs open and the commerce flowing.

Whatever type of venture saw them far from home,
They had to deal with elements across the mighty foam,
Hail now to our mariners going west across the Bay,
The Portland stone awaits - on your return one day.

Sept. `06

BILL THE GUNNER

The soldier fought hostilities with bayonet and the gun,
To take a life was always thus since modern wars begun,
The airman dropped his bombs, knew not the number killed,
Sent aloft in aeroplanes where `ere his bosses willed.

The sailor fired from battleships, sending men to doom,
Or delivered death by depth charge with underwater boom,
All the fighting services were trained in what they do,
Stood for King and country and all that's right and true.

Alas the Merchant Seaman aboard his sitting duck,
Steamed about defenceless unless he had the luck....
To have an anti-aircraft gun mounted on the deck,
Perchance to hole a bomber `afore it made a wreck.

Officials issued Orelikans, a Vickers or a Bren,
Usually pretty ancient, unfamiliar to our men,
They were taught the `hose-pipe` method - in a sort of sermon,
And it wasn't very easy to shoot a flying German.

But I knew a certain Captain - the Skipper of a trawler,
Patrolling down the East coast, he shot `em down to order,
As his score just mounted, the Navy mused how high,
For when the foe approached him, he shot `em out the sky.

He was pressed to give a lecture before the convoy started off,
To a bunch of gunner ratings and a Royal Navy toff,
The Skipper wasn't quite prepared as he rolled in through the door,
So said he'd answer questions from that lot on the floor.

It was the ribboned Admiral who spoke and said like this;
“Skipper, pray please tell us, of how you rarely miss,”
’Tis easy said the Master, we don’t fret at all,
I send to get my Mate out - he’s a man whot likes a brawl.

“There’s another coming Bill,” I sez, “go shoot the bugger down,”
So he ups and mans `is orelikan with conceytrated frown....
`Cus he tends to wait a bit `till he sees the pilot guys,
Then `e sprays`em in the cockpit - an` right between the eyes.

That’s the one that gets `em , `an puts `em off their stroke,
They nose dive to the water in a cloud of spray and smoke,
I winks at Bill and throws the chalk - so `e can keep a tally,
And mark the ones we’ve blown up, `an sunk there in Bomb Ally.

THE BO`SUN

The Bosun’s legs were damaged, swollen black and blue,
Chief Steward quite bewildered not sure what to do,
Consulting then the Captain they studied up the guide,
(A special one for Master’s to take advice inside).

This Captain’s Medical Guide covers all the ills,
Tho’ instructions are ambiguous for serving drugs and pills,
There’s cures for mental illness, scalds and having babies,
Plus fevers, burns, athlete’s foot, drugs, alcohol and rabies.

The Captain was quite practised, his duty wouldn’t shun,
Reckoned he had it cracked it, knew what must be done,
They had sailed from Argentina the weather hot and red,
Said the right thing for the Bo’sun was cool him in his bed.

Stack his legs with frozen cubes, were orders to his crew,
All hands mostly happy now, knowing what to do,
The Chippy made a special box to fit this man precise,
Shoved the Bo’sun’s limbs in, then filled it up with ice.

The Chief worked hard with spanners to keep the fridges purring,
Night and day maintained away – to make the frost occurring,
Steaming through the tropics they looked after him with pride,
Chilling down the Bos'un on his scorching ocean ride.

He lay there in a stupor as he followed this routine,
Of frequent shots of rum while piling ice between,
They finally reached Cape Verde and put the man ashore,
Bunkered then with booze and fuel, sailed again once more.

Most mariners are hardy – go through life with ease,
Not troubled much with ailments or tropical disease,
Till the ship received a cable saying
“ Bad news I`m afraid

Your man expired of frostbite……… when ninety in the shade".

DISRESPECT

I won't forget seafaring men that lost their lives at sea,
With unremitting courage they sailed for you and me,
The Channel and the Med. - Russian convoys too,
North and South Atlantic, where `ere the ensign flew.

The far off Indian Ocean and our coastal routes,
Anywhere a U- boat - points her tubes and shoots,
Torpedoes striking ammo - heard three hundred miles away,
Or tankers full of petrol in firestorm hell display.

Laden craft with iron ore - their plates just blown asunder,
Engines pounding full ahead, driving them straight under,
Other ships took longer, but lethal just the same,
Sinking with their lifeboats or going up in flame.

It was each merchant vessel, with a doughty crew,
Strove to keep its cargo, boldly steaming through,
A quarter of our seamen were sent to Neptune's hold,
Their resting place is sacred below the waves enfold.

Now it seems that divers, on a desecrating spree,
Found some tombs of seamen and it's clear to me,
`Tis not a leisure pastime or treasure hunting game,
But disregard to brave men and thoughtless evil shame.

Relatives and veterans demand that common law,
Stop this wicked practise near the ocean floor,
Leave our reluctant heroes to their endless sleep,
Not disrespect our Seamen and make the angels weep.

SAILING AWAY

The parting sun sends out a glow across from Walton Bay,
Westward then we're bound to go battened down - away,
It is the Western Ocean lads - that's the road I'll tread,
Sailing from old Bristol port to clear my lubbers head,
To mighty seas and howling breeze strumming a bracing song,
A voyage round on a `city` boat - that's where I belong

JOHN`S DAILY WALK

I step out every morning down a country lane,
Spy the little birds, the moor hens and the crane,
Perhaps a climbing squirrel or lazy grazing horse,
While ambling round the village on my observant course.

I often spot a seagull gliding low across the land,
This takes me back across the years – seamen understand,
I may recall of earlier times when down the River Plate,
Or when I was a Tanker man sailing off Kuwait,

Steaming down to Rio and Recife on the way,
Surfing Roaring Forties and round to Botany Bay,
Suzy San in Kobe where I spent some time,
Warmer climes of weather `an crossing of the line.

I think of all those ladies that were so cute to me,
Departing sad but keen to go when I returned to sea,
I sit down for a breather, and watch the Mum's school run,
Thrusting buttocks pushing prams, to this old man it's fun.

I arrive back home again my walking voyage over,
Day dreaming of my early days as a seamen rover,
But still I have that feeling – that latent, blatant urge,
To sail away to sea again, the landlocked air to purge.

Thoughts from my brother John while out walking.

THE STOKEHOLD

I passed a big ship steaming - into a heavy sea,
Powered by steam engines - to some a mystery,
She had a `woodbine` funnel forcing up the draught,
So I knew the `Black Gang` were working at their craft.

Trimmers kept fuel coming, with barrows full of coal,
Often from the `tween-deck `an the vessel on the roll,
Firemen fed the furnaces making constant steam,
Choking and half roasted, eyes smarting to extreme.

Several of those ovens under their command,
In non-stop roar of engines and boiler's fierce demand.
Attired in vest and blue jeans, sweat rag duly clutched,
Leather belt worn backward or buckle seared when
touched,

Iron doors hinged open - facing fervent heat,
An art to shovelling coal trying to keep your feet,
Raking and a`poking to stop clogging of the bars,
Sweating bodies shining over tattoos and the scars.

An eye upon the gauges to keep things just precise,
Striving with their working tools - devil, rake and slice,
Used to sort the clinker out `afore eight bells applied,
Trimmers hauled the ashes up and dumped `em overside.

Well beneath the waterline these men earned their pay,
Supplying red hot caverns, two hundred tons a day,
I passed that big ship steaming - many years ago,
Knowing that her `Black Gang were slaving down below.

THE WILSON LINE

When a young man in my prime,
I shipped aboard the Wilson line,
From Hull to Denmark on a regular run,
Ideal voyage - lots of fun.

This suited married men of course,
Not long away so no remorse,
Fine home port and one away,
One with wife `tother to play.

Our fine crew with liberties taken,
Shacked up too in Copenhagen,
Things were fine for a year or two,
Then one night - right on cue.

Policemen raided O` dear me,
Forty girls put on the quay,
Headline news in Danish paper,
Also Hull heard of the caper.

The crew would now be skinned alive,
(Including me there were twenty five),
We paid off on board in secrecy,
I pondered on the plans for me.

The Marine Super was no fool,
He shipped me out of Liverpool,
I heard things later - in due course,
About the bust ups and divorce.

But when she signed a brand new crew,
There were willing men in a lengthy queue.

(Roughly as told to me by my brother John)

RAY PEARCE M.N.

1925 – 2004

He never mentioned it before, not until this year,
Never wanted to – it disturbed and sprung a tear,
Torpedoed there in one ship – he had not told a soul,
When recalling his old shipmates in a dreadful waiting role.

For he was in a lifeboat with sixteen other men,
A few of them were injured – could do nought for them,
One of them was badly burnt, within his roasted skin,
Memory so traumatic – he'd felt so much for him.

He told a bit to you guys – now the time has gone,
These men died in agony departing one by one,
Two days in a lifeboat – death reigned there supreme,
Ray, he was not injured, but a lad of mere sixteen,
(From an interview in 2003 with Ray and Age Exchange of London).

There were many unsung heroes in the war at sea,
This is one example – for it seems to me,
They carried out their duties, neither bragged nor spoke,
Seafarers with the Nelson touch – and mighty hearts of oak.

Feb. 2004

The 6 O`CLOCK SWILL

(In Australia/New Zealand)

Remember the `Down Under swill boys, when pubs were shut at six,
With only half a dog watch to drink our daily fix,
We grafted all day to earn our pay – seamen in our prime,
`Taws five p.m. `afore allowed to spend our social time.

With schooners of beer in excellent cheer we joined the other Abs,
From various craft with motley crews arrived from overseas,
The Shaw Saville ships or Blue Star and tramps the likes of Hain's,
Among the vessels loading, or discharging under cranes.

Ale was shot into glasses from a tap on the end of a hose,
Held in a crate and paid for straight – then thrust to under your nose,
Our favourite tipple went down well, swilling and drinking apace,
Too soon, to soon, eight bells were struck – we had to get out of the place.

Carry out, carry out, the cry goes up so we ordered the best on the coast,
With beer on our hip and away from the ship we followed a willing host.
We revelled then and had our fill – perhaps stayed there 'till morn,
Kissed the sheilas, bid farewell and back on board by dawn.

Another hard day but on the way to repeat a fine night a shore,
Showered and shaved in no time – then straight for the bar-room door.
So if you recall the fifties and the six o'clock swill like me,
Do you remember Auckland and 'Ma Gleesons' by the quay?.

St. STEPHEN`S WINDOW

There's a holy place in Bristol - St. Stephen's it is known,
One time called the Harbour Church, for it stands within the zone,
Abeam of Bristol's centre where clippers used to moor,
When the bustling river, once lapped upon its door.

There is now a stained glass window, facing to the South,
To honour local seamen that sailed from Avon's mouth,
Depicting the red ensign, plus the navy blue,
Below the Merchant navy crown and the reef knot too.

You may glance to Heaven, as you intone a prayer,
Perchance to see this tribute to seamen everywhere,
To remind us of all souls that braved their life at sea,
And those reluctant heroes that died for you and me.

CONVOYS

Our lads that sailed in convoys – officers and ranks,
Deserve a special mention and our heartfelt thanks,
Most vessels were quite sound – manned by crews well trained,
Others were the opposite, most scrap and rusty stained.

These doughty merchant seamen knew their cruel fate,
When struck by cunning sea wolves lurking there in wait,
If they lived to tell the story and strived to stay afloat,
They struggled then with hardships aboard an open boat.

Still they served our country sailing there and back,
Hauling vital cargoes in times that looked so black,
A dangerous job in peacetime they continued just the same,
During war at sea my friends – through the shock and flame.

Course it was the ammo ships that were blown to smithereens,
While plodding past the periscopes of hidden submarines,
Also on the tankers - one hardly had a chance,
When spotted by the enemy re-armed out of France.

The mines were pretty lethal, lurking God knows where,
Happenchance to strike one – turmoil then and there,
The bombers stretched to reach `em had a bit of fun,
Dropping tons of dynamite against a paltry gun.

Then there was the weather, with storm and hurricanes,
Very near impossible to steer intended lanes,
Especially wild Atlantic and freezing Russian run,
Casualties horrendous `till the job was done.

There was a school of thought – to foil the U-boat ace,
Just give the Royal Air Force some extra fuel space,
In long range Liberators to patrol as ocean scout,
Instead of burning cities and knocking civvies out.

Later on this was done – though several months too late,
Condemning many cargo ships with their precious freight,
Gradually the sinkings were cut by lessons learned,
Though still appalling losses until the tide was turned.

So crucial were these convoys to the war by land and air,
There's a mighty debt to seamen that served for us out there,
They paid the price of liberty by standing firm and fast,
And still we fly their ensign - stubborn from the mast.

SAIL-ON

Sail on my friends, in convoy`s keep,
Leave me here in the deep to sleep,
I watch you go midst bubbling wake,
You will not stop – too much at stake.

Sail on old friends, my ship`s gone down,
It won`t be long before I drown,
Tell my loved ones – all that knew me,
Torpedo`s target – lost at sea.

Sail on my friends, you may survive,
Our vital cargoes must arrive,
Take a drink if you reach port,
Remember me – give us a thought.

Steam on young seamen – go full speed,
Our Country`s at its greatest need,
I give my life for others bread,
Farewell mates – now I`m dead.

THE FREEDOM OF OUR CITY

The freedom of our land men, the freedom of our land,
Now we think of doughty men and how you made a stand,
Our country really needed you when called on to defend,
It's that you fought and died for, 'till the bitter end.

The freedom of our seas boys, the freedom of our seas,
You carried on your duty boys, sailing from the quays
Ranging round the world in peace, also in the wars,
You reluctant heroes, hauled succour to our shores.

The freedom of our city lads, the freedom of our city,
For you Merchand Navy lads – who brought prosperity,
In Bristol's recognition – and at the peoples bid,
Take honour from our citizens recalling what you did.

On the Merchant Navy being granted the freedom of the City of Bristol.

July 2002

THE STANDARD BEARER

I am a standard bearer, I'm striding mighty proud,
Conscious of my posture as I pass the cheering crowd,
My standard is a tribute - represents the men,
Who served and died for country, plus veterans since then.

You may see the likes of me, with gloves and belt so white,
Leading homage with my colleagues in uniforms alike,
Since the Romans with their signum or vexillum toting rag,
There has been a `banner bearer` with his special flag.

An honour and a privilege I do the job for free,
I ask no fame or kudos nor princely sum or fee,
Unabashed to shed a tear at funerals where I go,
I'm thinking of my freedom and debt I surely owe.

I stand tall at the functions, or freedom of a city,
The cenotaphs, or marching, where bands beat out a ditty,
Tis fitting and my duty - while the last post sounds ahead,
For me to dip the standard, remembering the dead.

Dedicated to all Standard Bearers - inspired by `Wings` Barry - Bristol Branch M.N.A.

LUCK

West of the Scottish Orkneys in October '39
A flotilla of our battleships steamed along in line
The Navy's grey destroyers patrolling on the flanks
When a U-boat prowler found itself among the ranks.

It was unbelievable, a chance was heaven sent
A great attack position, found without intent
Right ahead was Rodney, then the Nelson and the Hood
A full supply of tin fish – but none were any good.

From the German submarine, torpedoes hit their mark
Incredibly those duds, never caused a spark
In disgust the Captain - Lieutenant William Zahn
Lowered down his periscope then submerged and ran.

It was a great embarrassment to the Donitz Kriegsmarine
Aboard the flagship Rodney were V.I.P.'s supreme
Sir Dudley Pound and Churchill with other Admiral guys
Engaged on board for parley after Royal Oak's demise.

I would call it fortunate at that time of the war
When underwater weapons sometimes failed to score
There was no doubt about it – a dangerous place to be
So lucky for the top brass and First Lord of the Sea.

There were 31 U-boat attacks from favourable positions, four attacks on the Warspite, twelve attacks on various cruisers, ten attacks on destroyers and five attacks on troop transports. All torpedoes failed to explode.

FARED WELL

Along the road of memory I wander now and then,
I hear the wind, I smell the air, I'm sailing once again,
I'm pacing on a sturdy ship with land a distant view,
Recalling of my younger days, worries but a few.

Laughter filled the morning watch, seafaring was my joy
When I was young and able for I was just a boy,
Now my body's failing I see a twilight sky,
The sea is in my blood still, at least until I die.

Salt water has its way - has done over years,
In some form or another - often sweat or tears,
I have lived a happy life - no regrets for me,
With loving wife and children plus travelling round at sea.

I'd like to tell my family when I leave them all alone,
Please forgive these ramblings of when I used to roam,
For you are in my mind right now, as I rue my destiny,
I'll carry on forever, you are my immortality.

Soon I'll cross the bar, for sure my time is nigh,
My turn has come my friends, to bid you all goodbye,
It's nature's way, no worries - look,
Just scribe `Fared Well` in my Seaman's Book.

OLD VETERANS

In bloom of life they sailed away,
At sea along with peers,
They kept the lifelines flowing,
Amid the U-Boat fears.

There they lost their shipmates,
That never did grow old,
Though veterans remember,
As advancing years unfold.

They saw the perils of the deep,
The best and worst in men,
Grieving with compatriots,
In the war back then.

Now these reluctant heroes,
For them no grave the deep,
Progressively they cross the bar,
A rendezvous to keep….

THE T.S. INDEFATIGABLE

They travelled up from villages, the city and the fen,
Young lads sent to `Inde` to train as sailormen,
Most were only fourteen – raw or streetwise youth,
Some from broken families, all of them uncouth.

Arriving at this training ship upon the Menai Straits,
Embarking on a tough regime once passing through the gates,
Instilled in them a discipline learning all the while,
Comradeship and fortitude to go that extra mile.

There was no mollycoddling while gaining self respect,
Marching to a bugle band and drummers beat erect,
Torn away from apron strings, standing quite assured,
Confident and able, afore they went abroad.

Sitting on old Nozzer`s Rock they never will forget,
Reflecting on the values they'll also not regret,
The vista of Mount Snowdon across the other shore,
While manning up the whalers and pulling on the oar.

Rodney, Drake, Raleigh, Hood were divisions there,
Leading hands and head boys served a handy share,
Supervised on navy lines by officers and peers,
The making of our seamen, all throughout the years.

Developing a character bringing to the fore,
Reliant sturdy mariners in times of peace or war,
Eventually they sailed away – began a life at sea,
Joining ranks of hardy souls with `Inde` pedigree.

Many served as Captains, others came ashore,
All of them indebted for biding there before,
Recalling all the standards and qualities back then,
That set the course of youngsters and turned `em into men.

P.O. Boy J.Earl No. 98 Hood Division Jan. `56 – July`57.

THE PADDLE STEAMER `BARRY`

Cheers to the pleasure steamer – popular and fast,
With a jaunty rake of funnel and bunting from the mast,
Paddles swooshing easily foaming as they churn,
Leaving wake – ruler straight, trailing there astern.

Her glossy shining paintwork of red and pearly white,
Flying proud the ensign on halyard whipping tight,
The cheering of the passengers leaning on the rail,
And jingle of the telegraph when about to sail.

The fascinating engines steaming hell for leather,
Captain's orders from the bridge open to the weather,
Called upon in wartime years for such sterling work,
Plus helping out the Navy and Army at Dunkirk.

One such vessel of renown was the ***P.S. Barry,***
Famous in the Great War for troops she had to carry,
Outstanding in Gallipoli and last from Suvla Bay,
Serving at Salonika toiled in danger's way.

She was built upon the Clyde one hundred years ago,
Excursion fit for passengers on deck and down below,
Registered in Barry - in her early years,
Calling in the Channel ports mooring at the piers.

Ilfracombe or Weston, down to old Minehead,
Burnham and the Mumbles - then home in time for bed,
She gave so many people, hours of bracing pleasure,
Merrymaking families enjoying days to treasure.

Later on in `twenty-six she worked our southern climes,
Sailing out of Brighton and Hastings many times,
Then sweeping mines in `forty-one on a fatal run,
She perished in the North Sea, sunk there by the Hun.

It's right recalling history of South Wales long ago,
Of local crew and seamen sailing to and fro,
For they worked the paddle steamers giving them their power,
In our favorite waters – from Bristol to the Gower.

The Paddle Steamer Barry was built for the Barry Railway Company's fleet and sailed on May 24, 1907, before leaving the Clyde to begin her pleasure steamer career from Barry and the Bristol Channel.

2007

THE SAGA OF THE FLYING ENTERPRISE 1951

It was the *Flying Enterprise* steaming to the west,
Her Master, Captain Carlson, was about to stand a test,
Christmas day in `51 he met a violent storm,
Standing out in history greater than the norm,
Days and weeks she hove-to, in heaving seas of green,
Tossing, wild and pitching, cracks on deck were seen,
In this mighty hurricane she rolled her beams close under,
And structural damage evident began to break asunder.

Four hundred miles past Lands End an S.O.S. was sent,
To save the crew and passengers now the ship was spent,
The troop ship *General Greely* came upon the scene,
And the Yankee steamer *Southland*, nearby on the beam,
They could not launch the lifeboats, the list was too severe,
So jumped into the water as rescuers pulled near,
Ten passengers plus crew were saved, chilled through to the bone,
Leaving Captain Carlson aboard there, all alone.

Battered by the giant waves, to port she heeled and listed,
Included in her cargo was pig iron, which had shifted,
Forty-five degrees or more she lurched and there she stayed,
Failing then to right herself, on her side, she laid,
A deep-sea tug, the *Turmoil,* eventually came by,
The Mate of her, Ken Dancy, in a case of do-or-die,
Leapt aboard the stricken ship to give a helping hand,
Aiding Captain Carlson and his vessel far from land.

Those two men together in a Herculean task,
Hauled a cable inboard and made the tug all fast,
Steadily they towed her, slowly, every day,
Till closing near to Falmouth forty miles away,
The weather worsened once again then the tow-line parted,
Ship`s demise now obvious our heroes broken hearted,
Walked along the funnel, as it was laying flat,
Made it to a lifeboat, and that, my friends was that.

Two men well remembered for an epic of its day,
Maritime tradition and bravery held sway,
The sea's a haughty mistress and frequently takes charge,
Testing all our seamen and mariners at large.

LIBERATE THE FALKLANDS

The Time has come the British said – to back up our demand,
Travel to the Falkland Isles and then reclaim our land,
Maritime logistics and forces set in motion,
Took the war eight thousand miles across the mighty ocean.

Invincible and *Hermes* were the aircraft carriers,
Protected by our warships - and a couple of dozen *Harriers,*
Troops were sent on *Canberra* and the *QE 2,*
Fuel and stores on merchantmen where the duster flew.

Admiral Sandy Woodward and Sea Lord Henry Leach,
Commanded this armada and landings on the beach,
Below the waves our submarines watching all the way,
Sinking one big cruiser, then kept the rest at bay.

The `Junta` sent the *Exocet* and *Super Etendard,*
Skyhawks and the *Daggers* were held in high regard,
Battles that were fought where the Argies made a stand,
Varied from the bombing, to fighting hand to hand.

The army did the yomping when their transport sadly sunk,
When Cunard`s *Conveyor,* was hit and turned to junk,
Commandos and the Paras, went the extra mile,
Over barren countryside steadfast all the while.

Avro Vulcan bombers served us very proud,
Winging back from Stanley after strafing through the cloud,
A record set in history for the longest bombing flight,
Proved a masterpiece of flying, through the day and night.

Galtieri showed his arrogance and made a bad mistake,
Thinking that old England would it's land forsake,
We lost a lot of brave men, some aeroplanes and ships,
Fully laden landing craft suffered dreadful hits.

But the Air force and the Navy, Army and Marine,
Carried out their duty to Country and the Queen,
And the Merchant Navy, under our red duster,
Special - indispensable when armadas have to muster.

Again reluctant heroes when the nation needs to fight,
Our sturdy unsung mariners showed their worth alright,
So raise a glass to *Stanley* where once a white rag flew,
And all the ships that sailed there with a hearty crew.

Vital Need for Merchant Ships - *Up to the surrender in mid-June, 40 merchantmen totalling over 500,000 grt reached the South Atlantic. Without them, the war would not have been won as the Royal Fleet Auxiliary lacked the ships to transport the land forces and then support them and the warships 8,000 miles from home.*

PHILIP ZEC

On the outbreak of the 2nd. World war Zec was commissioned by the Daily Mirror do a daily cartoon. Zec's cartoons were an immediate success with the readers. Zec, who was Jewish felt passionately about the need to defeat Hitler, produced a series of powerful cartoons on the war. When Hitler heard about these attacks on his regime, he added Zec's name to the Nazi Black List of people to be executed after Britain's defeat.

Zec sometimes upset the British government with his cartoons. On 5th March, 1942, the Daily Mirror published a cartoon on the government's decision to increase the price of petrol. The cartoon showed a torpedoed sailor with an oil-smeared face lying on a raft. Zec's message was "Don't waste petrol. It costs lives."

"The price of petrol has been increased by one penny." Official (5th.March 1942)

Winston Churchill believed that the cartoon suggested that the sailor's life had been put at stake to enhance the profits of the petrol companies. In the House of Commons, Herbert Morrison the Home Secretary, called it a "wicked cartoon" and Ernest Bevan the Minister of Labour, argued that Zec's work was lowering the morale of the armed forces and the general public.

Churchill arranged for MI5 to investigate Zec's background, and although they reported back that he held left-wing opinions, there was no evidence of him being involved in subversive activities. The government considered closing down the Daily Mirror but eventually decided to let the newspaper off with a severe reprimand.

THE S.S. DAYBREAK

Nineteen seventeen it was – during perilous days,
The freighter S.S. Daybreak loaded deep with maize,
Steamed along on Christmas Eve near the Southern Rock,
Off the coast of County Down abeam of Strangford Lough,
No notice or forewarning, a torpedo found its mark,
It came and blew the nose right off – plunging all in dark
The vessel's screw rotating during its descent,
Her boilers then exploding as underneath they went.

U – Boat Eighty Seven had loosed her lethal load,
To meet this helpless target on a winter's ocean road,
One and twenty brave men - the total of her crew,
Murdered in the Irish Sea by folk they never knew,
It was seen by witnesses or perhaps we'd never know,
What occurred to brave men dragged down far below,
Entombed there now forever, thirty fathoms deep,
Akin to unsung mariners in Davy Jones's keep.

RAYMOND VICTOR STEED

A Galley Boy named Raymond Steed joined the `Empire Morn`
At the docks in Newport, close where he was born,
In The Merchant Navy now - but only just fourteen,
He'd gone to sail in convoys - fighting fit and keen.

Nineteen forty three it was, aggression in full flow,
Unmindful of the danger, he couldn't wait to go
Ray carried out his duties, earning meagre pay,
Until alas in April, his world was blown away.

Not far off Casablanca, the `Empire` struck a mine,
Laid there by a U-Boat with purpose and design
The consequent explosion, set cargo blasting then,
Killing brave young Raymond and twenty other men.

His body's in Morocco, near the road to Marrakesh,
In a nurtured cemetery surroundings trim and fresh,
He was the youngest Seaman, to go and lose his life,
While standing firm in jeopardy mid the wartime strife.

Greater than five hundred boys, were sent to Neptune's floor,
Sixteenth birthdays never met, lost for evermore,
They helped sustain our lifelines in a hostile time at sea,
Those young and unsung heroes that sailed for you and me.

SPECIAL EMBLEM

I watched our Standard flutter gently in the breeze,
Saw the duty bugler positioned there at ease,
Soon then at attention – everyone was still,
Then I heard the bugle sound and felt a sudden chill.

It's a very special emblem our Standard-Bearer carries,
Born aloft with deference where good men meet at rallies,
Gathered in a meeting place in homage to our dead,
It represents raw courage, on oceans far widespread.

Dipped in hushed remembrance while standing on parade,
In unison with `last post`, or `sunset` when it's played,
Reflecting on our brothers at the bottom of the sea,
The unmarked tomb of mariners - freedom is not free.

Worn upon our merchant ships not only when we muster,
It's the mark of British Seamen, who call it our Red Duster,
Sometimes at a funeral it makes a coffin shroud,
A final sad reminder that a veteran's served us proud.

For centuries it's been displayed, time has not forgot,
When nobly then it sailed with us into the shell and shot,
I watched our ensign flutter gently in the breeze,
And wiped away a tear - when the bugler stood at ease.
Inspired by `Wings` Barry - M.N.A. Standard Bearer.

BARRY SEAMEN

Many Barry seamen, during world war two,
Lost their lives on colliers but hardly given due,
Mostly served as firemen down the engine room,
Along with hardy stokers and trimmers in the gloom.

In dungarees and singlet they toiled there in the heat,
Well below the waterline to a rolling beat,
They did not have much prospect, working there below,
When a U-boat shot his tin-fish and set the ship aglow.

If perhaps they made it and scrambled up on deck,
Wearing gear I mentioned and sweat rag round the neck,
They faced the cold Atlantic, storms, or raging fires,
Perchance to gain a lifeboat afore the ship expires.

Even then, against the odds, if rescue's carried out,
Pay was stopped without delay leaving kin with now`t,
They were unsung heroes and defence was mighty thin,
Waiting for a big bang, and plates to crumple in.

Per head of population Barry lost the most,
Of hardy merchant seamen from around our coast,
In Holton Road a monument, stands for all to see,
A tribute to those brave men who sailed to keep us free.

BARRY DOCK - LOADING COAL

Barry Dock was opened in eighteen eighty nine,
Crucial was the need, at that specific time,
Exporting coal most everywhere, Barry had no peer,
Exceeding even Cardiff, along the coast near here.

From pits within the valleys, the black stuff rumbled down,
By railway through to Cadoxton and on to Barry town,
The owners sent the captains with their empty ships,
To load these bulky cargos, underneath the tips.

The collier pumped out ballast and gangway put ashore,
Then took on her freight, with a dusty crashing roar,
One by one the coal trucks were emptied down the chute,
While hard men trimmed the vessel and cargo holds to suit.

Finished off and loaded, the Mate would note her draught,
The crew turned-to, washing down, hosing fore and aft,
Shifted to a lay-by berth or mooring side by side,
Battened down and ready, to sail the ocean wide.

Agents and the chandlers, seen bustling back and fore,
Across the dock, the boatmen, sculling with an oar,
Tugs hooted out their signals towing craft about,
Most sailing or arriving until the tide ran out.

Time maybe for a pint or two in the old `Chain Locker`,
With a tattooed shipmate, or local friendly docker,
Twice a day locks were manned, around high-water mark,
Pilots sent to waiting ships, ready to embark.

It wasn't just the coal cargoes that made the place well known,
A fine repair and dry dock was famous on its own,
Grain mills and a cold store stood nearby on the land,
Ammunition loaded, fire brigade on hand.

Vessels moored at anchor, from Breaksea Point to Sully,
Till summoned by the Dock Master always in a hurry,
The Port was home for many ships travelling blue highways,
And the best of Merchant Seamen, in those yesterdays.

THE ARMY / SOMME

MY DAD`S WAR

My Father Frank Earl was born in 1895

When the first world war broke out - with the patriotic fervor at that time, Frank joined as a volunteer and then commissioned as 2nd. Lieut. On 28th. Nov. 1914

On 10th Sept. he enlisted at Sheffield Corn Exchange with the Sheffield City battalion - the 12th B. York and Lancaster Regiment, consisting of University and commercial men as well as men from all walks of life. Between 900 and 1,000 men were recruited in 2 days.In December the battalion went to train at Redmires camp, west of the city for 5 months. Training then followed at Penkridge Bank camp nr Rugeley, Ripon,and Hurdcott Camp near Salisbury throughout 1915.On 20th Dec.the battalion left for Alexandria Egypt on HMT NESTOR as part of the 94th Brigade.(31st division)

They had been assigned to defend the Suez Canal, but threats of an attack by the Turkish army diminished, and the Division was sent to the Somme. On 10th March 1916 they embarked on the crowded ship H.M.T. BRITON at Port Said, other ships were torpedoed nearby but they reached Marseilles on 15th.March. They then had a 15 hour train journey and a 12 mile route march to Pont Remy near Huppy. 18 days later the battalion took over a stretch of the front line opposite the hill-top village of Serre. The Sheffield City Battalion were at the extreme left of a 15 mile front defended by the British, stretching south from Serre to Maricourt.

On Saturday 24th June, the British artillery opened a bombardment that over a 5-day period was intended to destroy the German defenses completely. Each night the battalion sent out raiding and wire-examining parties; ominously, the German wire was found to be incompletely cut. On 28th June, word was received that the attack would be postponed for two days because of the poor weather. The new time for the start of the offensive was 7.30am on Saturday 1st July.

At 3.45am on 1st July, the battalion was in position in the assembly trenches, finding them already in an atrocious condition from German shellfire. Patrols from the 4th and 7th Companies of the 169th (8th Baden) Infantry Regiment defending Serre noted the build-up. With the appearance of daylight at 4.05am, German artillery began to shell the British front line.

At 7.20am the first wave of the battalion moved 100yds into No Man's Land and lay flat on the ground as the brigade mortar battery and divisional artillery placed a final hurricane bombardment over the German front line. A few minutes later - with the British front line coming under an intense counter-barrage - the second wave took up position 30yds behind the first.

At 7.30am the bombardment lifted from the German front line. All four waves rose, took a moment to align themselves, then advanced steadily towards the German lines into a devastating hail of machine gun bullets and shellfire. An ineffective smoke screen exposed the battalion to machine gun fire from the left as well as from ahead. The third and fourth waves, caught on the opposite side of the valley, were reduced to half strength before even reaching No Man's Land. On the left of the battalion front, long stretches of barbed wire had been left uncut. Men brought to a halt in front of the impenetrable entanglements were reduced to firing vainly through the wire to the German lines beyond. Some managed to return to the British lines. Others were never heard of again. Within minutes it was as if the battalion had been wiped off the face of the earth... The battle for Serre was lost.

My Father was shot in the first wave at 0730 He lay out in no man's land with all the shelling and machine gun fire. Within minutes only remnants of the battalion were left, and were taken out of the line on July 3rd, having lost 513 officers and men killed, wounded or missing, and a further 75 slightly wounded.

Of 36 Officers and 747 other ranks that went over the top that morning, 18 officers and 495 other ranks were casualties – out of the 248 officers and men killed 165 were never identified.

Throughout the Battle of the Somme, Serre was never captured, falling into British hands only in 1917.

After the war Sheffield placed a memorial in the village of Serre to the men of the City Battalion who had fallen in the attack of July 1st 1916.

My Father, Lieut. Francis Campion Earl, (age 21) was wounded, (he was a bomb thrower) lying out in No Man's Land for several hours until dusk. He had severe injuries caused by shrapnel in his chest and a bullet wound in his abdomen. He took a lot of aspirin, and a cat came and sat on his stomach whilst he was lying there, keeping him warm. He was rescued - with others - by his Sgt. Major and a group of men, and sent back for treatment for peritonitis, and a damaged kidney (which had to be removed.) and liver, and later developed an abscess in the right groin. He was evacuated to a little hut where first aid was carried out and then to a big house for further attention, he was then evacuated to a hospital at Le Treport, where his mother and brother were sent for, as he was so dangerously ill. He was incapacitated for military duty for 4 months. He left Le Havre on 6th august 1916 on the ASTURIAS, arriving at Southampton on 8th August 1916 and travelling to 2nd Western General Hospital, Manchester. He joined the 3rd Bn Yorks and Lancs on 2nd Nov. 1916.He was appointed Temp. Captain while Adjutant of a Volunteer Bn in 1917. His wounds caused problems for him and he eventually relinquished his commission on completion of service from 27th Jan 1920, being granted rank of Captain.

When the 2nd world war was declared the Local Defense Volunteers were soon formed.

Dad organised the local villagers and they used to drill with sticks on the lawn. He was made Company Commander of `B` Company 2nd. Bn. Sherwood Foresters Home Guard responsible for the area Retford to the Trent at Dunham Bridge.

They were fairly well trained and even captured a German airplane pilot who had bailed out.

My Father died in January 1946 at the age of 51 he had 7 children – I was the youngest but one and only four and a half years old when he died.

THE MENIN GATE - YPRES

There was an awful tragic feature of the First World War,
Captured here in `Wipers` at it's city door,
Only names remain in a chiselled state,
Lasting long in testament upon the Menin Gate.

Once these words were soldiers, husbands, brothers, sons,
All to perish somehow if not by hungry guns,
The telegrams delivered - though the heart was stilled,
A little hope perhaps when `*Missing - Believed Killed*`.

The last ray then extinguished when welcome peace reborn,
There was no grave to visit - outlook so forlorn,
No resting place to shed a tear or token left above,
Just a void of sadness and abject grieving love.

The Salient kept its secrets - guards it's very own,
Few individual crosses or inscription set in stone,
So then was built a monument to mark the episode,
Topped with British lion looking down the Menin road.

Mention by a poet - popular at the time,
He called the arch a sepulchre and put it down to crime,
For the carnage of our forces - the total number stuns,
Still it was not big enough though twenty thousand tons.

At unveiling of this monument the Generals made it clear,
"*These soldiers are not missing - they are resting here*"
In memory of our dead, vanquished in that fight,
We stand to heed the `last post` - sounded every night.

Blomfield`s memorial combines the architectural images of a classical victory arch and a mausoleum and it contains, inside and out, huge panels into which are carved the names of the 54,896 officers and men of the commonwealth forces who died in the Ypres Salient area and who have no known graves. This figure, however, does not represent all the missing from this area. It was found that the Menin Gate, immense though it is, was not large enough to hold the names of all the missing. The names recorded on the gate's panels are those of men who died in the area between the outbreak of war in 1914 and 15th. August, 1917. The names of a further 34,984 of the missing - those who died between 16th. August, 1917 and the end of the war, are recorded on carved panels at Tyne Cot Cemetery, on the slopes just below Passchendaele.

THE BUGLER

Our Bill played the bugle, our Bill played `Last Post`,
Bill came through the `Great War` - luckier than most,
Lance Corporal William Turner - his proper name you see,
Fought there in the trenches with Highland Infantry.

Playing over battlefields on sodden mud landscapes,
He sounded off at burials - frequently his mates,
Bill was knocked about a bit, by one exploding shell,
The same that killed his General - so played at his as well,

Later on in `83 he returned nearby once more,
Bringing back his bugle - the one he played before,
Standing at the cemeteries with tearful shining eyes,
He paid respect to colleagues - his battalion guys.

Now this year his Daughter - Peggy Tolfree came,
With her Dad's old bugle, turning out again,
To visit battle graveyards and the Menin Gate,
Where you'll hear the `Last Post` for men who met their fate.

There is a certain romance between a Bugler's call,
And a stirring memory that people may recall,
A rallying cry or death knell - whatever it may be,
It's men like William Turner that bring it home to me.

Nov. `04

LOSS

I'm standing by some poppies and rusty piles of ammo,
Near sunken ditch and trenches, filled in long ago,
Blue sky stretches over, the skylarks soar aloft,
The open space of no-man's land ploughed in furrows soft.

Where once brave men of Britain and the hommes of France,
Were slaughtered by the foe in defending or advance,
They lost their lives for duty and family there at home,
Amid the shells and bullets in lethal honeycomb.

Widows left bereft, mothers broken hearted,
Brothers and the sisters all forever parted,
We shall never know the cost - by way of things undone,
No marriages or offspring taking natures run.

Untold loss of futures that never now will start,
This demise so precious, impossible to chart,
Such result of war - the consequence so bad,
No wonder that I'm standing here, so beset and sad.

D-DAY - ARMADA
Operation Neptune

Rank after relentless rank they came,
Facing guns, bombs and flame,
Six thousand craft, ten lanes wide,
Advancing in the ripping tide.

Seven hundred warships too,
Armed and set with a job to do
Fast mine sweepers at the van,
Fighter squadrons weaved and ran

Twenty miles across the beam,
The greatest convoy ever seen,
Endless columns of surging craft,
Landing ships with shallow draft,

Liners, ferries, packed with troops,
Attack transports, army groups.
Barrage balloons on display,
Spread across this vast array,

Red Cross vessels, laden tankers,
Ancient tubs missing anchors.
Coast guard cutters, motor boats,
Painted out in grey topcoats.

Channel steamers, out from Dover,
Modern freighters steaming over,
Winking lights as morse is spoke,
Rusty coasters belching smoke,

Swarms of tugs, rolling tramps,
Packed with stores, guns and tanks.
They sailed this day for liberty
To crush the foe and set us free.

D - DAY June 6th 1944

I went to view the battlefields of Operation Overlord,
Fifty miles of coastline from Utah Beach to Sword,
To gain a hold in Normandy, D- Day was the key,
A step to free all Europe and beat Hitler's Germany.

We marshalled all our forces after well-honed drills,
Comprising all resources with their special skills,
Twelve thousand allied air planes, three million men and more,
Land and sea and airmen determined to endure.

A convoy of six thousand, steamed across the sea,
From warships to assault craft, burgees flying free,
While our Paratroopers, jumped to hold the flanks,
Heavy Naval gunfire supported all the ranks.

Resistance here was mighty strong through the hostile surf,
They fought and strived side by side to gain the foreign turf,
There are many tales of bravery and yarns of daring do,
Bad luck or just good fortune - plus error factors too.

Steaming through old minefields, making life quite fraught,
Mulberries were towed across to make a discharge port,
For berthing of the liberty ships - seven at a time,
While Operation Pluto was the laying of pipeline.

The planning and arranging a monumental slog,
This final push to victory a mortal heavy job,
Supplies proceeding quickly - another fine endeavour,
Though there was a setback, provided by the weather.

This Normandy invasion was the biggest undertaken,
Embarked upon with allies - confidence unshaken,
I paid respect with colleagues at the wonder of the plan,
And the acts of courage displayed by every man.

Paid homage in the graveyards as I took my tribute strolls,
Faced the plaque at Arromanches for Merchant Navy souls,
We will not forget them - history points the truth,
On the altar of our freedom brave men gave their youth.

April `04

THE ULSTER 36th. DIVISION 1916

Early on Lord Kitchener inspecting on the Green,
Stated that the Ulstermen were the finest he had seen,
They were the Irish rifles and the Royal Fusiliers,
Including Inniskillings and the Tyrone Volunteers.

On July the first the `big push` saw the Irish troops,
The Thirty-sixth division, opposing German groups,
Many miles along the Somme our boys stood the test,
Ulster's proud division making up the best.

Facing stiff defences from Schwaben`s tough redoubt,
The Ulsters fought for high ground `mid carnage all about,
Feats were incomparable among the spilling blood,
Achieved by unsung heroes, in that foreign mud.

Silencing machine guns, fighting hand to hand,
They took the German trenches - there they made a stand,
But then trapped in a salient when distant flanks were lost,
Suffered fire on three sides at enormous cost.

Companies were wiped out, the Ulsters carried on,
Over dead and dying, they reformed and fought along,
Soldiers caught in enfilade, shellfire did for more,
Still this brave division held on at the fore.

Dreadful though the outcome, foundations now were laid,
The enemy was shattered by harm the Ulsters made,
On went the day so lethal, for objectives seized,
That won acclaim for gallantry including four V.C.s.

A tower stands in County Down, where lads trained for glory,
Near Thiepval Wood a replica, built to tell the story,
Of the red hand badge of courage and fighting all the way,
And the sacrifice of brave men - for peace we have today.

MY PALS

We sailed from old England across the grey sea,
Gaining the beach at French Normandy,
In a dip in the soil I looked around,
Seeing our Fred smacked to the ground,
Then I spied Harry bloodied and still,
Alongside a mate, alas it's poor Bill.

Shouting us on, our tough Sergeant Bruce,
With holes in his helmet and arm hanging loose,
Onward and upward we tried to gain cover,
Hearing a young man crying for Mother,
There were blinded and limbless spread on the sand,
Some calling for medics to give `em a hand.

Loaded with backpacks the going was tough,
Shooting and running we made for the bluff,
Soon I found Tommy shot through the neck,
The havoc and carnage continued on yet,
My colleagues, my friends, comrades in arms,
Dropping like flies with guns in their palms.

Too many men I have known for so long,
Lay wounded or dead or simply just gone,
We fought on the grounds - in from the sea,
For freedom, for God, for whole victory,
I do so remember - will never forget,
My pals from old England - laying there yet.

THE BRIDGE OVER THE RIVER KWAI

I travelled far in Thailand – to heat like a Devils brew,
The steaming hellish cauldron that soldier prisoners knew,
When made to build a railway, along the River Kwai,
Many men were sent there, many were to die.

Withstanding Jap and jungle they laid an iron trial,
Each sleeper rates a body, left to tell the tale,
Days were long and cruel beneath the Nippon whip,
Malaria and dysentery - no mercy for the sick.

Wearing only rice sacks – no shoes on flinted stone,
Ulcers were abounding, rotting to the bone,
Nights were spent in attap huts with two foot six of space,
Soon to shouts of `Speedo` work resumed apace.

Cutting out the Hellfire Pass, building trestles on the way,
Nearby making quotas - one thousand yards a day,
By hand they hauled the timber, from the woods around,
Digging up the bamboo, levelling out the ground.

They built a bridge to fall down named the Pack Of Cards,
Risking death and torture from barbaric guards,
Sabotage was carried out as the structure grew,
While enduring dengue fever, beri beri too.

Hard then to imagine the soldier's state of mind,
As they saw the rail to Burma though the hills unwind,
Relieved to have it finished – an end to mortal toil,
But not to see the enemy shift their troops and oil.

In the Soldier's graveyard that mark those bitter years,
Inscriptions on the stonework witness many tears
For here the foreign visitor found time will not appease,
Strange though something's missing – the tourist Japanese.

In June 1942, 61,000 British and Allied troops were put to work by the Imperial Japanese Army to construct a railway line 415 klm. long in mountainous terrain to link Kanchanburi in Thailand to the railway network in Burma. (To supply their army there, thus avoiding the hazardous sea route around Singapore) First estimates by the Japanese suggested it would take at least 5 years – under tremendous pressure the P.O.W.s were forced to build it in 16 months at the cost of 16,000 lives.

WE REMEMBER

As I wait beneath the trees,
Softly kissed by gentle breeze,
Pigeons, gulls and swans abound,
While our veterans gather round…

By water's edge - just sublime,
Then recalling fraught war time,
Assembled here for all to see,
For those that fought at Normandy.

Lucky us this summer's day
We do remember - let us pray.

At the Merchant Navy Association Monument
6th. June.

GATHERED HERE

Once again gathered here - we count the cost and flow,
Of those that crossed the bar - the men we used to know,
Although perhaps we shed a tear at setting of their sun,
Let's celebrate the life they led - a voyage home now run.

In battles lost with foe, or ancient year's last mile,
It's how a life was lived that makes a man worthwhile,
Those that went some time ago, we remember still,
Upholding debt of gratitude boding no one ill.

Others gone more recently our grief we now defend,
A legacy astern - for nought goes with us in the end,
For each of us our day will come, and then your God may say,
"Welcome Shellback, come aboard - your friends are left to pray".

THE BATTLEFIELDS

I can see the battlefields all around the Somme,
Remnants of old scars, left by shell and bomb,
I can see the plains - flat and waterlogged,
Overlooked by slopes the crafty foe once hogged.

Imagine man's despair in the trenches` sodden mire,
Enduring waiting hours grieving under fire,
Biding with the rats and constant itching lice,
In amongst the `whiz bangs` that slaughter in a trice.

Chewing on Maconochies – perhaps a shot of rum,
The honing of a bayonet and wiping of a gun,
From a distant ruin, a sniper plays his game,
Leaving postured corpses stiffened by his aim.

Craters in the mudscape, barbed wire stretched as well,
Appalling pong of rotting horse and explosive's acrid smell,
Miles and miles of carnage making stark morass,
Over there, creeping green, ghastly mustard gas.

I wonder at the fear with bullets all around,
On a likely rendezvous with death on foreign ground,
The haggard desolation in the face of every man,
For the taking of a shilling to join the General's plan.

I can imagine soldiers tense on timber deck,
Waiting for a signal – the whistle round a neck,
Scrambling up a fire step to charge there over top,
A rattling of machine gun - then a sudden stop.

I can see the battlefields – no war or guns are there,
Just a skylark singing – peaceful in the air.

OUR SOLDIERS

You wear the kevlar helmet when going on patrol,
Code signs on the flap sheet when warriors start to roll,
R.P.G.s incoming - expecting all the time,
Contact with Insurgents or deadly roadside mine.

You Tommies toil in searing heat and dust forever there,
Living out of bergens and flies are everywhere,
Stags of sentry duty `neath a sanger`s roof of tin,
The cutting edge of combat and training kicking in.

You lads ain`t amoral and get on with the job,
Have a kind of system when a mortar does a lob,
Engagement rules are rigid in those stinking lands,
Dicing with the petrol bombs hurled from children's hands.

All the gear – no idea, is how you see the Yanks,
But occasionally you owe `em one and nod to give `em thanks,
For coming in with air support in their classic style,
Helping out when `danger close` in a horror riven mile.

We know it makes you angry when media get it wrong,
But the public is behind you – has been all along,
Sometimes it aint that easy, to share a point of view,
Unless it's with a mucker that's been through same as you.

Years from now like other wars – the difference is of age,
Your work is relegated to films or history page,
But for now in infancy thinking more of home,
The bind falls on your loved ones – when they put down the phone.

Joe. Earl R.E.M.F.

MISCELLANEOUS

SPORT OF KINGS

There is a grace and beauty of a racehorse on the run,
The champions outstanding and galloping for fun,
Giving all and battling `till the race is won,
These mighty beasts have heart - names trip off the tongue.

The monster *Barracuda*, the ease of *Never Say Die,*
The silver *Desert Orchid* as he passed his rivals by,
Red Rum - a triple winner upon the National course,
My favourite *Persian Punch* a stubborn gutsy horse.

The spirit of *Sea Biscuit, Arkle* and *Mill Reef,*
The wonder of old *Generous* who beggared all belief,
The steeplechaser *One man*, the famous *Golden Miller*,
Dawn Run on the chases with *Jonjo* at the tiller.

Partnered by the jockeys - adding magic to the game,
Gordon Richards, Lester Piggot heading list of fame,
Followed by *Dunwoody, Francome* and *McCoy,*
Thornton, Tizzard, Murphy and *Fallon* since a boy.

Cheeky *Frank Dettori, Carson* of renown,
Riding out from places like Lambourn county town,
Where Mum was once a stable girl spreading youthful wings,
In among the characters that made the sport of Kings.

TO CHRIS

Hello Chris – I give you this – to Hell with the expenses,
It is a little thank you – for sorting out my tenses,
Sorry 'bout the Handbag verse – thought I had just cause,
Shall I write another one – about the menopause?

But do you want all hands to know? – not just only me…
Perceiving of your antics while popping HRT,
Rolling round with night sweats and flushing of the boobs,
Combining with extremities of violent swinging moods.

No, I think I'll keep odes gentle, 'tis better far when printed,
Then read 'em all like me – through glass a little tinted.
So I'll pick a friendly subject – when inspiration led
Like the one about the lamp-post – that hit you on the head!

Love Joe
August 2002

CONCORDE

Concorde, Concorde, Bristol's bird,
Her sonic boom no longer heard,
A pity though and sad for us,
Next best thing is a flying bus.

We marvelled at our speedy dart,
Assembled here in state of art,
Engines thrusting just sublime,
Scudding high before her time.

Born with dreams this super ride,
Built with vision flown with pride,
Far too young to be too old,
Shelved at peak not to be sold.

Many fans are saddened now,
Since our beauty took a bow,
We will remember - won't forget,
Our graceful, wondrous, world's best jet.

Nov.2003

NATHAN

Nathan is a little boy - I reckon three feet tall,
Sometimes in a temper - he chucks breakfast at the wall,
`Tis hard to have a chat with him, when he nods his head,
He could not say just `yes` or `no` as this is what he said;
"*I'm not talking now Nanny - I've lost my no's and yesses"*
Fortunately he got `em back - now yes and no expresses,

We took him to a car-boot sale in the local fields,
He loved to look at little toys - most of them with wheels,
He wants to see again, now he's earned some brass,
"*Mum"* he said, *"let's go, to that shop on the grass"*.

May `04

PILLS

My brother John frequently forgets to take his pills for his various ailments so I sent him a poster sized verse he can stick on his kitchen wall to remind him as follows:

`Tis good, Old Man, while living life to reject your ills
I'm not a Doc but it helps a lot if you take your ruddy **pills**

He replied;

I read your note about my ills
Remember now to take my pills
But I found on sad reflection
I forgot to take my injection
I can't help it if my memory's gone
But thanks a lot - your sister John.

JAKE'S DOG

My favourite grandson Jake, yearned for a canine chum,
He pleaded with his dad and often asked his mum,
Eventually and happily there came that wondrous day
A puppy from a litter – a pet was here to stay.

They purchased bowl and basket, for it to snuggle down
And bought a pooper-scooper on the way from town
Then both impressed upon him, now he owned a mutt
He's the one in charge of it so keep the front gate shut.

Jake listened to the lectures on what he had to do
Promised he would train it and find it bones to chew
Father bade "look after it" pointing with his fork
"Don't forget" warned mother "you'll take it for a walk".

Even when they go away arrangements have been done
Granddad's taking care of it – he can have some fun
Asked about the collar – what name should we engrave
"Why" said Jake just smiling – "I think I'll call it Dave".

Dave the dog!!

August 2002

THE REASON

There is a point of reason – any time of season,
To think about or write a bit of verse,
I may rhyme a bird of feather
With a bank of yellow heather
Lo an unseen hand just changes tack

Other bards may grace waving fields of corn
I would rather tall ships, sailing round the Horn
They write of mighty oaks or spreading chestnut trees
My mind is of tea-clippers, scudding in the breeze.
They picture golden daffodils – I fully understand
While couplets come to me, of seascapes far from land.
They imbue their flowered pages – sketch the babbling brook
While seamen and the oceans deck my weathered book.
Since Noah rode the flood – I reckon true in part
The sea is in the blood – if a Mariner at heart.

THE PUB

Oh woe is me the powers that be have closed my local boozer,
Such a shame – the brewers gain but I'm the poor sad loser,
No more at will a swift half pint when I'm feeling dry,
Or a dirty joke an' a bit of wit with a fellow minded guy.

For many years I've propped the bar with only yards to stumble,
The nearest now is miles away – no wonder that I grumble,
I'm full of tears, I have my fears aboard a tipsy bike,
It's such a way, and I must say, the walking I dislike.

Our crib team and the darts, lifeless, dead, defunct,
The village heart and soul is gone, an' the skittle ally junked,
I feel so sad it's just too bad at the way it has to be,
For I miss my pub (and it's grub) – it was just like home to me.

Filthy and full of strangers!!!
Summer 2002

CHRISTMAS

Christmas time on the Welsh Back
A boy was standing there
His Father was lost in the deep
The lad was saying a prayer

"I love the presents and holly
All the fun and the glee
But what I truly wanted
Was Dad by the Christmas tree

So please take care of all seamen
Especially for children like me
Make it a jolly fine Christmas
With Dads home safely from sea".

THE EX PATS

Ex patriots they scamper off – they go to live in Spain.
For to escape the fog and cold depressing rain,
The house is sold with furniture and garage sales abound,
The car is filled with personal stuff as they steam from
Plymouth Sound.

The Costa Blanca beckons them with a new life to the fore,
With a brand new villa waiting or apartment with pine door
But take heed my friends and listen before your all is lost
In case with heavy heart old son you must count up the cost.

The cloudless skies and burning sun – in relentless way,
Remember you're an Englander – do you want it every day?
It's a lazy life and so laid back on a pool side plastic chair,
Time to think of family and wish they too were there.

But it's not to be, then you see your life's been split asunder,
Time goes on in relaxing mode but still one has to wonder,
Of a normal day in a northern zone with seasons of the year,
Where the weekend days are different and all your friends
are near.

A million brits are out there on the Blanca or the Sol,
For some the Spanish good life takes a weighty toll,
It's not my imagination – for I came out to see....
And speak to many ex-pats an' it's what they told to me.

For plenty it is perfect – I've no call to shout,
But if you're set on moving, please have a shade of doubt,
For I came, I saw, I pondered, by the Mediterranean sea,
Found so many amigos would fly home with me.

Voya en casa manana

INSPIRATION

How often have I started out, no verses in my head?
Perhaps while eating breakfast or buttering my bread,
When something will occur to me, though maybe
lacking glamour,
So toil to set the rhyme out, and probably the grammar
Consulting of the dictionary, try to sort the tenses,
Shape it all about a bit - appeal it to the senses.

But now and then while boozing,
Words don't need such choosing
My poem then - so refined
Sits perfect healthy in my mind…

But then next day it comes to nought,
I`ve disremembered every thought…

When I'm sober.

SNORING

Sometimes I slumber at your side - me of ceaseless hum,
You're very good, seldom chide, though you would I dumb,
Moo`ing like a cow for aid or the grunts of swine,
The noise all night cascade, through that nose of mine.

A screeching storm around a crag or bellow of raging bull,
The cry of an injured stag - then a sudden lull,
Now the din is back again like a ship about to sink,
With the roaring main, over the bulwarks brink.

The rumbling of an earthquake, the whistling through the rigging,
The screaming that a plane makes, all the banshees singing,
Throughout, vibrations start up, to the Richter scale,
While turning in my cart - this heavy slumbering male.

I sympathise, as you give a growl, trying to find release,
You hear a dingo's howl then squirm there in your fleece,
Upside down in swaddling clothes to avoid the clatter,
Waking your beloved - he utters *"what's the matter?"*

Your love for me now here it tells.....
Putting up with my decibels.

MANDY

Rene has a little dog - I think her name is Mandy,
She wears a coat in rain and fog - it makes her feel quite dandy,
She's a terrier from the Highlands - I s'pose she is a Scot,
She really loves the children and plays with them a lot.

She is a trifle lazy, now she's getting old,
But who could really blame her for not walking in the cold?
She is a special guard dog and a very special pet,
Even though she barks a lot - I haven't heard her yet.

It's only at the postman or school kids up the road,
Or perhaps the noisy milkman delivering his load,
So Rene cares for Mandy `cus she really is a winner,
Then Mandy's very happy and gets `Bonus` for her dinner.

YOU WILL LOOK SEXY AT SIXTY

(To one of my female friends)

Oh you will be sexy at sixty,
Of that I'm perfectly sure,
Like a good tune on a fiddle,
Best when played mature.

A woman will stare in a mirror,
Sees what she wants to see,
I'm not being kind - it's all in the mind,
You are what you want to be.

Remember the urge of early days,
Before so cosily wed,
Many a touch and plenty of ways,
While sexily sprawling in bed.

A man likes a lady with style,
No matter the age of her rings,
One that has lived for a while,
And knows incredible things.

You don't need the limited span,
Of an urgent and selfish boy,
Find on old man with a devious plan,
To bring you rapture's of joy.

You ***will*** look sexy at sixty,
I'll tell you the reason you see,
I am the beholder and quite a bit older,
You'll ***always*** be younger to me.

THE WAITING IS OVER

(On my Marriage to Chris Aug. 20th `05

The waiting is over our day's here at last,
Though stretching through summer it's come very fast,
Chris helped me along - put wind in my sails,
No nasty hic-ups like the poor Prince of Wales.

Nice to see Norman with banner unfurled,
The girls are so gorgeous - the best in the world,
Champagne's not real but tastes just the same -
I could get used to this marrying game.

Finally spliced I'll get on with life,
With loving and caring and beautiful wife,
Just living and joking to bring a nice smile,
Then flying away to flop for a while.

We are not doubters we're perfectly sure,
We have all we need - and a lot more,
Togetherness now - no longer apart,
`An I'm popping the pills to feed my old heart.

Bless both our families and Heaven above,
For the life that we have - so filled with love,
We'll steam full ahead - make best of our times,
Betting on horses and writing some rhymes.

So thank you from us with tears in our eyes,
Enjoy yourselves now - `till we say our goodbye`s.

BARBADOS HONEYMOON

We splashed about in turquoise seas
On golden sands we browned our knees
Glimpsed the turtles break for air
Pastel shades everywhere
Now and then perhaps some rain
Fell until the blue skies came
Tinkling sound of metal drum
A little taste of local rum
Hearing bits of Bajan song
Nothing hurting nothing wrong
Resting `neath our tamarind tree
Happy there - you and me
Golden isle in perfect bliss
Loving you - my girl Chris.

CHRISTMAS IN SAND BAY

Christmas Day in Sand Bay one of great delight,
Mostly quiet from early morn 'till kids wake up and fight,
One may see the dog walkers, on our beach so wide,
In amongst the flotsam that came in with the tide.

There is a smell of cooking from houses and some flats,
Leaving scraps for pets and all the feral cats,
No more merry parties in our pub that's shut up tight,
Now a barren wasteland, like a building site.

Sand is blowing everywhere, the air is really fresh,
Everyone with anoraks to heat the crinkly flesh,
I doubt it will be snowing, but loads of gales and rain,
Hiding in the clouds, the frequent aeroplane.

You may just see a straggler escaping from the camp,
Maybe on the wall – if the wheelchair climbs the ramp,
'Cus they had their Xmas dinner way back in July,
Pulling all their crackers, 'neath a summer sky.

You often see a local horse, pass a place like mine,
Blocking off the road and crapping all the time,
Manure is then collected before it's all squashed flat,
It's for chucking on the rhubarb and other stuff like that.

There is a festive feeling as I walk along the lane,
The red lights round the doors and twinkling window pane,
Nice artificial holly made of paper, string and felt,
I'll be wearing mistletoe – I shove it in me belt.

THE MOLE

I work hard in my garden,
to keep well manicured turf,
Weeding and trimming all over,
slaving a bit like a serf,
Now there’s a mole in my haven,
it tunnels right under the lawn,
I reckon he favours the night shift -
leaving big mounds there at dawn.

It started off in the corner,
then followed the patio’s edge,
Zigzagging a bit to the middle,
keeping away from the hedge,
I scratched my head and got angry,
at the wreck of my grass displayed,
Guessed the spot he was digging -
then rendered him dead with a spade.

GIRL`S NIGHT OUT

(On my granddaughters Friday night)

We're getting ready - nice and slow
Almost there and time to go
Chatting on the mobile phone
Usual gang so not alone

Hair is sleek and shining too
Left wet towels in the loo
Make up nice and strappy top
Tartlet skirt and glow sticks rock

On the floor - boys around
Deejay's club mix is the sound
Getting smoochy with the guys
Maybe give one - a surprise

Supping up the vodka ice
A couple of shots - very nice
Stilettos pinching starting blisters
Wicked fit boys - for us sisters

Dancing then `till night turns grey
Grab the purse and on the way
Hugs and kisses all around
Singing still now homeward bound

Farewell lads it's been great fun
Got to go now - have to run
Do it all again next week
Working off our rebel streak

Make up nice and strappy top
Tartlet skirt and glow sticks rock.

BIRNBECK ISLAND PIER

This ancient rock still proudly stands,
Mid`st ebb and flow by Weston Sands,
In its heyday host to steamers,
Calling here decked out with streamers.

Entertainment – high spring tides,
Victorian evenings, lots besides,
Now my friends this is the story,
We`d like it back to former glory.

Connected to the land by pier,
`Tis been unused for many a year,
Except for answering mayday`s flare,
Brave men launching lifeboats there.

Let us too respond to calls,
Encourage life around its walls,
Give it heart and pulse anew,
Then stroll the pier – it`s good for you.

BIRNBECK IS A LADY

This island rock stands alone,
Empty buildings – no one's home,
Pity then the awful waste,
Like a lady too darn chaste.

Come my friends court her dearly,
Build esteem, bedeck her clearly,
Nurture her she'll glow and shine,
Beauty growing most sublime.

Such a phoenix from the ashes,
All embracing to the masses,
Along her pier, beloved, waiting,
Weston's jewel – scintillating.

MEN ARE PRETTY STUPID

Men are pretty stupid, this woman said to me,
Really? Please pray tell me – see if I agree,

"While we are discussing things he leaves and slams the door,
He doesn't know what housework is and dumps things on the floor,
Then he blames my hormones, if I'm a bit upset,
He can't remember anything – even where we met.

He doesn't like my cat and won't admit he's wrong,
Snores and farts in bed, just laughs when there's a pong,
He gives me good advice - feeling rather smug,
When all I really want is a warm and friendly hug.

He sulks and huffs and puffs if he doesn't get his way,
And he's always watching football mostly every day,
Will not ask directions even when he's lost,
Doesn't note my perm, no matter what it cost.

He often starts some DIY but fails to end the job,
Slaps my poor old backside when I'm cooking on the hob,
Has not a clue what flowers are – just cultivates the weeds,
Mostly turns a deaf ear when explaining of my needs.

He will not understand it when I need a pair of shoes,
And he's flicking through the channels while I'm trying to watch the news,
His Mother never trained him to lower the toilet seats,
And when he's had a bit to drink old jokes he then repeats.

He drives me to distraction – sends me quite insane,
Showing no emotion it's really quite a strain,
Never does the ironing, still I love the man to bits,
That's why men are stupid – wear the cap it fits ! "

BOB

Go in peace now old friend,
You kept a good watch to the end
Unselfish, brave, though growing old,
Your many deeds yet untold.

You served for freedom and at sea,
Lived a life as meant to be,
Loving husband thoughtful too,
Paternal, sound, the man we knew.

Uncomplaining, walking tall,
The best example to us all,
A leading light, a guiding star,
Farewell Bob – as you cross the bar.

Read at the funeral of my Stepfather Bob Arnott
October 2002.

WHAT SUMMER THIS?

What summer this if all the rain
Does not fall on Spanish Plain?

But drops on England's fertile land
Weeds and grass grow hand in hand.

The roads are wet in dim daylight
Stars obscured by cloud at night.

Children's play and fêtes are off
Colds abound with nasty cough.

One day perhaps, I hope it's soon
We'll feel the sun and see the moon.

What summer this without the fun
Of ice-cream, shorts and England's sun?

TIME FLIES

Heather is my daughter – she has three little girls
She also has a husband – a fair haired lad with curls
The eldest lass is Amy, she's very nearly ten
Her mum was born some time ago – I can't remember when.

The second one is Ollie, soon birthday number eight
Derek is her daddy and my good drinking mate.
The next one down is Jolie, the youngest and the last
And 'pon my soul' they're growing up so very very fast.

So when I'm old and eighty and the girls are gorgeous mums
Amy will be thirty-two (I've just done my sums).
Ollie will be thirty, perhaps she'll have some baby rascals
Jolie now at twenty-eight – well she'll still like bouncy castles.

They're all so nice and lovely, I'm sure they won't go wrong
And all the little kids they have will grow big and strong
Then when mum and dad grow older and go a little grey
They too can look forward to that very special day
When Amy, Ollie and Jolie have children of their own
But where are we going to put them? There is no room at home!

A HUMOROUS BREAK

I s'pose they call it `humorous` cus it's part of the funny bone,
Me - I hit the other end on a Sunday night at home,
A lovely day in every way `till I fell and struck my shoulder
On a very low coffee table, as hard as any boulder.

The morning was great, my girl was down, until she waved goodbye,
Then up to the Inn to view the sport - plus a pint with mates nearby,
Wandered home to cook my tea - made a lovely job of that,
My knee just went - sending me down with an awful sickening crack.

I've never broken a bone before - except the one in my nose,
Now there's a chunk out of my shoulder bone I regret now to disclose,
I don't mind the pain - it hurts when I laugh - or the fool that I made of myself,
But people assume that I tripped in my room - being pissed or drunk as an elf.

Not so of course but I'll stay condemned - though I never fell over before,
Between me and you I've reached sixty two - not once did I drop to the floor,
The reason I'm telling you this my friend - writing by hand is hard,
My arm's in a sling - can't move the damn thing - so I'm having a drink in the yard.

Dec. `03

WENDY`S REPLY

It isn't really funny,
When your mess-mates take the mick,
Laughing and a-sniggering
It's enough to make you sick!

For a change, you're totally guiltless,
You never did the crime
You only had a couple of pints
You didn't step out of line!

So slowly, from the New Inn,
You made your careful way,
You barely had a drop all night,
No matter what they say.

Accidents can happen,
As I'm sure you will agree,
Even to a sailor ,
Who's intent on cooking tea.

It's rotten luck it happened
When no-one else could see,
If you'd done it in the pub
They'd buy your drinks for free!

Now, it's not a joke , when your bones are broke
,'Cos the mess-decks unstable
Poor sailor-boy is home and dry,
To lift his pints, unable!

Our salty-tar has roamed the seas
From shore to shining shore,
The silly devil's knackered now,
He won't do that , no more!

So, cheer up, Joe we're sorry
That you fell, and are in pain
Please take it easy, just relax,
You'll soon be well again!

Best Wishes, Wendy.

REPLY TO 'YOU WILL LOOK SEXY AT SIXTY'

Hello, Joe, Here's a verse to say I'm living,
Not yet among the dead
Your honeyed words of flattery,
Have gone right to my head!
Your kindness means a lot to me,
So when I'm feeling low
Despite the squidgy, wobbly bits,
You'll still think I'm nice to know.

My ego has been massaged,
As a health cure, you're the best.
So, I've bought myself some scanties
And thrown away my vest!
I've gazed into my mirror
And primped and preened enough
Your words I'll sure remember,
When I'm feeling rough!

I've dolloped on the warpaint,
The wig , it is a winner,
I'm sure I've lost a couple of stones, '
Cos I did without my dinner!
My memory, it can fail me
At times I'm 'not quite there'
For I simply can't remember
If I'm standing on the stair,
Should I be going up for it? Or just come down from there?

Long ago it seems my yesterdays,
Were young and fancy free,
Bopping in the Cavern,
With a mini above my knee.
Long gone too, young Aussie gods,
Whose golden biceps rippled,
And the sultry Latin lover,
Whose sideburns I tickled.
Now, solid as a battleship
As in the days of yore,
I perambulate upon the prom
And SandBay's ocean shore
It's nice to know that you are there,
To smile and wave to me
Perhaps next time, you'll invite us in
To share a cup of tea!

LAUREN

We are so proud of Vicky she is a perfect mother,
We knew that after Nathan she'd want a sister for his brother,
Well she upped and managed it - I didn't ask her how,
But soon she bore dear Lauren, a lovely daughter now,
So cuddly and so beautiful you want to bite her bum,
Just like her mother's mother, has a little chubby tum.

LAUREN AT THREE

Lauren is a lady and a little fond of me,
She issues me with orders of how things have to be,
With curly hair and large brown eyes, she bends me round a finger,
To assist her with a busy task I must stay and linger.

She does a lot of talking, always asking why,
Listens most intently as she looks me in the eye,
While absorbing information I'm struggling to impart,
Careful what I answer, for it's taken all to heart.

Shaking head and smiling, with chocolate covered face,
Telling me what's nonsense to put me in my place,
She pulls me from my chair onto my dodgy knees,
To carry out her bidding at some instant wheeze.

With hands on hips to emphasise her words that must be heeded,
I carry on, her will obeyed, instructions best acceded,
I wouldn't mind - I'm sixty-four - but fine if you could see,
That Lauren's taken over - and she is only three.

Christmas 2005

GRANDAD`S KNEE

Nathan And Lauren and Joseph makes three
Think of the pain in Grandad`s old knee
So when they grow older and a bit overgrown
They will be sent to a chair to sit on their own
Better still yet it`s occurring to me
Lets pack `em all up and send `em to sea

TODAY'S CHILDREN

Mondays child will be a mugger,
Tuesdays child will maim another,
Wednesdays child will take to drugs,
Thursdays child will join the thugs,
Fridays child goes on the game,
Saturdays child will pimp the same,
The child that's born on the Sabbath day
Well `blow me down` it turns out gay.

SHIP HIGH IN TRANSIT

Manure was carried by sea my friend, many years ago,
Mostly dried and stowed in sacks in the hold below,
Often times in those days the ships did spring a leak,
Wetting fertiliser and causing such a reek.

Then began a problem - for it turned to methane gas
A single spark or candle flame, and up she went - alas,
Lessons then were learnt - so the stuff was stowed up high
Crucial now, important, to keep the cargo dry.

Marked upon the manifest and on the bags were writ,
`**S**hip **H**igh **I**n **T**ransit` - true origin my friend,
Of the word we know as ****

THE KITCHEN

I have a kitchen small and neat,
Preparing meals an easy feat,
Doings change for this poor man,
When lusted by the female clan.

For it used to be when fit and able,
I`d bend them `cross my kitchen table,
The ladies now have grown I fear,
Each one has a larger rear,

In the kitchen lack of room,
Kicking buckets and the broom,
Heaving belly like a fender,
Working on a fraught knee trembler.

Cups and saucers sent awry,
Spilt the gravy squashed the pie,
In amongst the screams and shouts,
Oops there goes the brussel sprouts.

In my galley self contained,
Passions clumsy unrestrained,
If designing kitchens do be sure,
To add at least a few feet more.

MY FAVOURITE THINGS

Pictures of convoys in arctic conditions,
Hearing the `*Last Post*` and bugle renditions,
The anchor engraved on one of my rings,
These are a few of my favourite things.

Paintings by children that turn out like doodles,
Teaching them how with drawings of poodles,
`*Wine Drinker Me*` that Dean Martin sings,
These are a few of my favourite things.

Brilliant ideas that come on in flashes,
Mending my p.c. after it crashes,
Girls in bikinis in hot water springs,
These are a few of my favourite things.

When my horse falls, when my luck swings,
When I'm feeling sad,
I simply remember my favourite things,
And then I don't feel so bad.

INJUSTICE

I feel for the men who have been cheated
The ones that went through the war
They fought for the process of freedom
And saw all the blood and the gore

They are strapped with a measly old pension
Though they rarely complain
Their pleasure is down at the local
In out of the wind and the rain

Say “good day” to the Landlord
And just settle down with a jar
Tamp on a pipe of tobacco
Relax and smoke in the bar

Now those bloody Do-Gooders
Have ruined the peace of the old
By making them stop what they are doing
And go out for a smoke in the cold

I reckon for all them true smokers
That laid their life on the line
It's a case of selfish injustice
And law ahead of it’s time

The heroes of England like Nelson
Would turn and revolve in their tombs
If they heard of the rule of no smoking
And insult added to wounds..

CHARLIE

I could have called him Sabre, Rex or maybe King,
He was a German Sheppard - a regal name for him,
But no, I called him `Charlie`, he answered to his call,
Big and black and beautiful, the proudest dog of all.

He guarded home and family, till I came home from sea,
Devoted and so loyal, he nuzzled up to me,
Later on, in old age, his hips would give him pain,
Then taking of his tablets he'd up and run again.

Eventually they wouldn't work, he flaked out on the lawn,
All night I kept him company, the pair of us forlorn,
It hurt too much to move him, we knew the end was nigh,
His love and comprehension looked me in the eye.

My pal, my friend, my trusted hound, I had to let you go,
That well remembered day - in May so long ago,
Nothing here on Earth, could make my sorrows drown,
That day I paid a local vet, to put old Charlie down.

WHEN I HAVE FLIPPED

When I have flipped this mortal coil,

Please spread my ashes among the spoil

On Sand Bay's beach in from the sea

I reckon that's the grave for me

OUR VETERANS

Once on the quay at Welsh Back, I saw our Veterans stand,
Time and care had reached them, over sea and land,

But now you'll see in passing, on seats erected here,
The nameplates of our heroes, in memory held dear,

They chanced their lives for country, asked not the reason why,
The Nelson touch abiding, within a sparking eye,

The long todays of youth soon pass, in this living game,
Tomorrows seemed so far away, they risked them just the same,

By sailing in our convoys across the devil seas,
Still our Duster flutters, because of men like these.

Joe Earl. Bristol M.N.A.

SAMUEL PLIMPSOLL

Good old Samuel Plimpsoll – he was the Seaman's friend,
He stood against ship-owners in order to defend
Basic rights and safety on all seagoing trips,
By bringing legislation to deadly `coffin-ships`.

A Liberal politician - a caring man for sure,
Born near docks in Redcliffe, in eighteen twenty four,
Long and hard in parliament he fought to have a say,
Eventually this Bristol man, won and had his way.

Excessive was the loss of life and so much common slaughter,
By sailing on decrepit craft too low in the water,
For many vessels left the quay, soon to sink right under,
Though well insured the cargoes of ships that broke asunder.

Men were thought expendable for the sake of profit,
Wicked were the ship-owners who made their money off it,
Countless crews protested all to no avail,
Refusing work on rotten ships – ending up in jail.

Many rights for mariners were plenty overdue,
Samuel saw at first hand so knew just what do,
He wrote about our seamen and perils shore to shore,
Urging for improvements and making them the law.

Soon the Merchant Shipping Act - of eighteen seventy six,
Demanded annual surveys, so measured marks affixed,
Upon the hull of all ships to denote a legal draught,
Assisting in the buoyancy measured fore and aft.

There is a bust of Plimpsoll, here in Bristol city,
A reminder yet of seamen of those he took such pity,
And homage to a great man in memory of those days,
When life was even harder upon our blue seaways.

MY GIRL

You're the kind of girl that men dream about,
You'll go out with me and still pay your shout,
Your sexy and loving and never come late,
Always thinking of me -your best mate.

And when we go shopping way up the road,
You never complain while humping the load,
Rarely a word `bout the gear that I wear,
Nor nag me about the length of my hair

You cuss and you swear while aiming the car,
Get on with my friends when down in the bar,
Let me go fishing though don't like the smell,
And bet on the horses - some donkeys as well.

You're my sort of girl that's plain to see,
You deserve a fair handsome romantic like me.

IT'S NOT FAR TO THE MOUNTAINS

It's not far to the mountains if distance made by crow,
Or the winding of the valley road snaking there below,
I'm lazing on our balcony looking to the east,
Soaking up the Spanish sun – troubled not the least.

An ideal spot for shellbacks recalling of the past,
Of life and love and glory days, most before the mast,
We sailed with our compatriots and harkened to the wise,
With convoy-hardened veterans, whose brothers lost their lives.

Youth, they say, is wasted upon the thrusting young,
I reckon not and no regrets while on the lower rung,
We romanced girls wherever, from Cuba to Japan,
Then bade farewell forever – goodbye fairy Anne.

I grin and drink my coffee, with a touch of brandy brew,
This long toothed pensioned seaman gazing at the view,
The goats and sheep go bongling past for their daily graze,
Reflections intermittent as I meet their ovine gaze.

So here in Andalucía, where the eagles soar,
A far cry from my tramping days and the breaker's roar,
I'm thankful for the memories and happy to review,
Till I take a cooling shower then light the barbecue.

THE SS ROBIN

Launched in eighteen ninety the Robin's fine design,
Made this old steam coaster a classic of her time,
She rolled and navigated, around our coast for years,
Driven by her engines and doughty engineers.

Replacing brigs and schooners she plied her salty trade,
Four hundred tons or more on a voyage made,
China clay or pit props perhaps a load of grain,
Railway lines or barrels she hauled `em just the same.

Later sold to Spaniards and then renamed Maria,
To roam the Bay of Biscay during her career,
She bunkered coal for liners, carried iron to France,
Dodging foe in wartime taking then her chance.

She was not big or glamorous but defied the odds,
Guided by her steering gear made of chain and rods,
Her end was very near, by scrap or fatal rust,
But luckily retrieved by an honest trust.

Now preserved in London moored up in the docks,
Serving as a gallery for promotions and workshops,
A triumph for our heritage especially maritime,
For she floats again as the Robin – and flies the red ensign.

THE PANAMA CANAL MULES

There was many a lad on a tanker, a liner or tramp of the sea,
That saved up bread for the `mules`, and one of those lads was me,
Informed by the crew it was routine, and nice to be such a pal,
By hoarding grub for old Dobbin, working the long canal.

For weeks while crossing the ocean, earning a Deck boy's pay
I stored all scraps and loaves there, plenty every day,
Later on, arriving, you could `knock me down with a feather`,
For it weren't the type of mule, with legs and reins of leather.

These beasts had ruddy big engines - a locomotive wide,
The game was up I knew it - I'd been taken for a ride,
Quick as a flash, in a hurry, I dumped my donkey stores,
Not acting like a lubber or a stranger to these shores.

I pretended I wasn't so stupid but wise to their childish game,
Patting myself on the back, for avoiding terrible shame,
But Galley boys and Peggy's that fell for the seamen's ruse,
Will never forget those mules - and bread they didn't use.

DAVY JONES`S LOCKER

I have sailed on mighty oceans and many a dangerous bay,
With Davy Jones a calling, inviting me to stay,
I thought then of his locker and contents of his deck,
Countless ships throughout the years sunk or made a wreck.

Fishing boats and tankers, missing submarines,
Once overloaded ferries and ancient quinquiremes,
Warships and the liners, planes without their floats,
Kon Tiki rafts and whalers and fancy motor boats.

Vessels deeply laden that never reached their goal,
Strewn across the murky wastes with ghostly silent soul,
The mast and yards of sailing ships pointing stiff and stark,
No use now to anyone, static in the dark.

Golden coins and cannonades, part of pirates` treasure,
Baubles from a Spanish chest sunken there forever,
Untold tombs of mariners and those that took a dip,
And many rusty anchors from craft that had to slip.

Cannon balls, gun barrels, bells made out of brass,
Dinner plates of sailors and portholes` rounded glass,
Wood has rotted slowly in places that we know,
Barnacles encrusting on iron there below.

The fishes keep them company, the massive whale and shark,
Giant squid and serpents, lurking in the dark,
I thought I'd turn his offer down – that Davy made to me,
Endeavour then to keep afloat – on Neptune's fickle sea.

FRED AND FREDA

We have a little casa out in sunny Spain,
Two hounds love to greet us, they live just down the lane,
Their names are Fred and Freda, they roam around the place,
Both are sandy coloured, of undetermined race.

Relaxing quite completely sprawled out every day,
We almost run them over as they natural bar the way,
They are so pleased to see us and wag their tails like mad,
Looking for their titbits with pleading eyes so sad.

Fred seems to be her bosom pal roaming free and large,
Freda is his mistress, smaller but in charge,
They hang around together, chasing cars an all,
Returning then to pant a lot in shadows of a wall.

Then one night a piercing cry, woke us from our dreams,
Fred had caught a neighbour's cat accounting for the screams,
We haven't seen our Fred since then – just Freda on her own,
Wondering if our Fred is tied, remanded there at home.

Later on we heard, our cheeky canine friend,
Had been a naughty boy, and met a sticky end,
He'd chased a couple of sheep and bitten through the fur,
Now condemned, regrettably, as a low down common cur..

Unfortunate our Fred did that, causing such alarm,
To us he was a playful dog that never did us harm,
I reckon that's just nature's way and Fred we'll sorely miss,
But we are still fond of Freda, and her big wet soppy kiss.

HE`S BURIED BY THE GREENHOUSE

He’s buried by the greenhouse - on his grave are flowers,
A family pet was Charlie, the memories are ours,
No more lead hanging down, by the kitchen door,
Or metal bowl of water, waiting on the floor,

No more friendly greeting, wagging of the tail,
Or barking at the postman, delivering the mail,
No more grinding jaw, gnawing bones of pork,
Or spinning in delight, at mention of a walk.

No more resting nose, gently on my knee,
Or limpid shining eyes, gazing up at me,
No more pleasant games, playing with a ball,
Or bounding back toward us, answering his call.

No more wet and smelly, after being in the rain,
Or the look of triumph, when he chased the cat again,
No more country strolls, sniffing round for hours,
He’s buried by the greenhouse now, underneath the flowers.

WHITE BERETS

They wear berets of white my friends, they wear berets of white,
For they sailed on Russian convoys, wondering day and night,
If they'd reach their destination in Murmansk further north,
Chancing Hitler's bombers or submarines sent forth.

Hauling vital cargoes men were sorely tried,
Carrying on regardless though many went and died,
Seventy-eight, the convoys that counted up the cost,
As there and back they lumbered, many ships were lost.

The wind would howl and shriek, round ice upon the yard,
In fog, snow and violent storms, life was pretty hard,
Plodding on laboriously, guarding round the clock,
Sleepless nights and piping cold until they reached the dock.

They risked their lives steadfastly, in dreadful bitter climes,
Long ago, but Veterans recall those vivid times,
That's why my friends I mention it, for they have earned the right,
To proudly wear a beret in the shade of Arctic white.

THE CALL OF THE SEA

In our island nation, within the shores of the free,
There is salt in the veins of our kinfolk and lust for life at sea,
Many seamen at home that swallowed the anchor back then,
Time and again have the urge, to pack their bags once again.

For they sailed out East through the Suez, to the far off Indian shore,
Or steamed off West with cargoes, to docks like Baltimore,
North in Arctic weather, through the snow and the ice,
Or Southern climes with palm trees and musky smell of the spice.

They kept a watch from the fo`c`s`le, an eye on the rise of the moon,
Or daylight trick at the helm `till eight bells struck at noon,
Sights they took with a sextant then pencilled a fix on the chart,
Or mothered the engines all constant, attending every part.

They heard the banshee screaming of storms sent over the deep,
Accustomed hard to seafaring, nursing the vessels keep,
Taking their fun and their fancy in ports wherever found,
Perhaps tattoos of a sailing ship inscribed with `Homeward Bound`.

They travelled the globe for months at a time over the ocean foam
Friendships forged of the lasting kind with men destined to roam,
Still the life of a rover, sometimes beckons to me,
I reckon its salt in the veins and the call of the sea.

A BRIEF HISTORY OF THE ONLY RUM WORTH DRINKING

On the 31st July 1970. The Royal Navy ceased to issue the daily tot of rum to their sailors. This day was dubbed "Black Tot Day" Rum had been served to ratings in the Royal Navy and Royal Marines serving in H.M. Ships and Establishments since 1665. It was indeed a "Black Day".

The origins of rum are shrouded in mystery. We do know that Christopher Columbus introduced sugar cane into the Caribbean over five hundred years ago. We do not know either where the name "Rum" came from, although it is thought it may derive from an old Devon word "Rumbullion".

The daily amount of rum issued in the ships of the Royal Navy, was determined by the individual Commanders in chief up until 1731. There was no accurate method of determining the strength of the rum either, so the effects on the sailors must have been variable also. In 1816 the "Sikes Hydrometer" was invented and used to measure the strength of all spirits with accuracy. But prior to this the strength of rum had been determined by mixing a few grains of black gunpowder with the rum, so that when the sun through a magnifying glass heated the mixture, it ignited. This was then designated the correct strength. (95.5 degrees proof (54.5% ABV), which is still the strength of "Pusser's Rum" blue label to this day).

The first regulated measure of half a pint per man per day was usually drunk neat. This resulted, as one can imagine, in a great deal of drunkenness amongst the crews. So it was that in 1740 Vice Admiral Vernon, Commander-in- Chief of His Majesty's fleet in the West Indies, ordered that the rum be mixed in the proportion of a quart of water to every half pint of rum. This was the mixture that became known as "grog" from the Admirals nickname of "Old Grogram", derived from his habit of wearing a coarse grogram cloth boat cloak. The rum was served twice a day by the ship's purser from a rum tub made from a "scuttled butt", a barrel cut in two.

"Purser" subsequently became corrupted to "Pusser" and of course that name is still in use in the Royal Navy to this day. In 1824 tea was introduced into naval rations while at this time the proportion of rum in grog had been halved to one gill (quarter pint) per day.

In 1850 a further attempt to reduce drunkenness was introduced, when the tot was reduced to half a gill, with compensating pay for an extra tea ration. This remained the official amount until 1970.

In 1979, Charles Tobias who as a boy in Canada remembered an uncle serving in the Royal Canadian Navy bringing home an illicit bottle of Pusser's rum, negotiated with the Admiralty Board and obtained the approval for the re-blending of Pusser's Rum to their original specification. He acquired the formula for the authentic Navy blend, which had never been previously available to the public. This was launched onto the market in 1980. Charles Tobias insisted that $2 per case sold worldwide would go as a royalty to the Royal Navy's tot fund in perpetuity. So if you want to help your comrades in the Royal Navy/Royal Marines, insist on drinking only "Pusser's Rum, after all it is the only rum worth drinking and is the official rum of the Royal Naval Association.

Printed in the United Kingdom
by Lightning Source UK Ltd.
130713UK00001B/1-111/P

9 781905 553303